MW01712486

BASEBALL STARS '82

BRUCE WEBER

SCHOLASTIC BOOK SERVICES
New York Toronto London Auckland Sydney Tokyo

Material for *All-Pro Baseball Stars 1982* closed on
December 20, 1981

The Author would like to express thanks to the American and National League public relations offices and the major-league team publicists for their help in assembling the material for this book.

Cover photo: Focus on Sports

No part of this publication may be reproduced in whole or in part, or stored in a retrieval system, or transmitted in any form or by any means, electronic, mechanical, photocopying, recording, or otherwise, without written permission of the publisher. For information regarding permission, write to Scholastic Book Services, 50 West 44th Street, New York, NY 10036.

ISBN 0-590-32392-X

Copyright © 1982 by Bruce Weber. All rights reserved. Published by Scholastic Book Services, a division of Scholastic Inc.

12 11 10 9 8 7 6 5 4 3 2 1 4 2 3 4 5 6 7/8

Printed in the U. S. A. 06

CONTENTS

Rickey Henderson — Oakland A's

American League All-Pro Team 1981

1B: Cecil Cooper
2B: Bobby Grich
3B: Buddy Bell
SS: Rick Burleson
OF: Rickey Henderson
OF: Dwayne Murphy
OF: Tony Armas
C: Jim Sundberg
RHP: Rollie Fingers
LHP: Ron Guidry

First Base

CECIL COOPER

MILWAUKEE BREWERS

The Boston Red Sox must still be kicking themselves. When they let Cecil Cooper go (for George Scott and Bernie Carbo) in 1976, they really didn't expect him to become the AL's regular All-Pro first-sacker.

Cooper has never hit less than .300 since he arrived in Milwaukee, including a .320 mark in '81 after a rousing .352 in 1980. And he's one of the premier glove men in the league, too.

Still, he isn't a household name — except in Wisconsin. The 6-2, 190-pound native Texan has always been in the wrong place at the wrong time. When he hit .352 in 1980, he picked the year that George Brett hit .390. Only four players in 30 years have hit .350 or better and failed to win the batting championship.

Cecil's luck began to swing right in '81. Clearly recognized as a hitter of merit, he even played on a winner for the first time. When the Brewers took the second-half title and qualified for the playoff preview round, national TV audiences had a chance to see the solid slugger for themselves.

One of the few lifetime .300 hitters in the game (.307), Cecil's ready to emerge from the shadows at age 32. After finishing among the AL leaders in doubles (first with 35), hits (third with 133), and runs scored (third with 70), he's ready to become a household word in lots of households.

Second Base

BOBBY GRICH

CALIFORNIA ANGELS

Statistically, the baseball players' strike of 1981 may be the greatest thing that ever happened to Bobby Grich. The Angels' second-sacker was rolling along brilliantly in early June when a fractured hand knocked him out of the lineup. Only a few days later, the strike knocked out baseball. By the time everyone came back, Grich was healed and his statistical dance picked right up.

The 32-year-old one-time Baltimore Oriole hit .304 for the season, including the league's top consecutive games streak (21 games, from May 21st to August 19th, spanning the strike). More important, he swatted 22 homers, tying him for the AL lead with Tony Armas, Dwight Evans, and Eddie Murray. He's the first Angel in the club's 21-year history to win even a share of a home run title. Bobby even won the AL slugging title. His .543 slugging percentage edged more famous sluggers like Murray, Evans, and Seattle's Tom Paciorek.

For the 6-2, 190-pounder, 1981 was easily his most successful year at the plate, though he had hit .294 with 30 homers and 101 RBIs in 1979. But when a lifetime .265 hitter has the kind of year Bobby had, everyone notices. And Bobby likes to play defense, too. "It's too bad that defensive players don't get more recognition," he says. "Unless you win a Gold Glove or set a record, no one notices."

Third Base

BUDDY BELL

TEXAS RANGERS

When the New York Mets were set to embark on their first season (1962), manager Casey Stengel was asked to name his rightfielder. The aging Stengel couldn't come up with the name until he said, at last, "and he rings the bell. And that's his name — Gus Bell."

Gus's kid, Buddy, is the big noise in the family these days. And no one has trouble remembering *his* name.

The Rangers' star third baseman is the steady hand on the sometimes-rocky Texas ship. Although he missed eight Texas games (he got into only 97), he still banged the ball at a .294 pace with 10 homers and 64 RBIs.

That Bell was selected as the AL's top third-sacker is a salute to his all-around play. After all, another third baseman, Boston's Carney Lansford, was the AL's leading hitter.

But Bell's stickout glove (he has a couple of Gold Gloves in his trophy case) and his timely hitting (his nine-game winning hits was tops among the Rangers) was enough to tip the balance.

A 16th round draft pick of the Indians in 1969, Bell reached the majors (as an outfielder) in 1972. He moved to third the following year. Now, at age 30, he has earned everyone's respect with his work at the Texas hot corner. Even Casey Stengel would have had no trouble remembering his name.

Shortstop

RICK BURLESON

CALIFORNIA ANGELS

When Rick Burleson joined the Angels (from Boston in December 1980), he said, "I'm going to play everyday, hit .275, and hustle all the time."

Unlike many players, he did even better than his promise. He played in all but one Angel game, hit .293, and, brother, did he ever hustle!

Though Milwaukee's Robin Yount battled Burleson right down to the wire for the AL's shortstop honors, Rick's consistent play did the trick. His former teammate, Jerry Remy, says, "No one comes to the ballpark with Rooster Burleson's attitude. He doesn't just want to do the best he can; he wants to do even better."

Good thing for Burleson that he played as well as he did in Anaheim. The three Angels who went to Boston in the deal for Burleson and Butch Hobson had super seasons. Carney Lansford, for one, won the AL batting title with a .336 average.

Still, the Angels didn't lose with Burleson. The 30-year-old from Lynwood, CA, has always been a solid glove man. He's the kind of guy who can settle the whole team in the field.

Rick's a team man all the way. "Sure I have personal goals," he says. "Everyone likes winning all-star awards. But I'd rather win the pennant than have a good year myself. I have this inner drive to do well. When I don't, I feel I'm letting myself — and my team — down."

Outfield

RICKEY HENDERSON

OAKLAND A's

Oakland manager Billy Martin always speaks bluntly. And when he talks about his leftfielder, Rickey Henderson, he gets right to the point: "He's the best player in the game."

Rickey is unique in a variety of ways. First, he bats right-handed and throws lefty. Most players with his speed prefer to hit lefty, giving them an edge getting down the baseline to first. More important, he combines his super-speed with one of the American League's best bats.

The 22-year-old hit .319 in his second full season in the majors. That was good for fifth place among AL batsmen. He was also among the leaders in runs scored (89), hits (135), steals (56), triples (7), and walks (64). Projected over a full 162-game season (the A's played 109), those numbers are most impressive.

In the field, he's even better. He made so many impossible catches last season, the A's stopped counting. The Oakland outfield trio all started as centerfielders. They're used to taking charge in the field.

Henderson was a star football and baseball player at Oakland Tech High School. (His junior year batting average: .716:) Though he could have become a great college running back, his mom advised him to play baseball. He made the majors within 2½ years. Now, every Oakland fan thinks Rickey's mom is a genius.

Outfield

DWAYNE MURPHY

OAKLAND A's

The A's patience finally paid off. Oakland has been waiting for Dwayne Murphy since 1973 when they selected him in the 12th round of the free-agent draft. Now, it appears, Murphy is ready to do the job for years to come. The pivot man in Oakland's super-defensive outfield, Dwayne has really responded to the teachings of Chairman Billy (Martin).

The 6-1, 180-pounder hit only .251 during the '81 season. But he swatted 15 homers and drove in 60 runs. Even more impressive was his consistency in the clutch. Fifteen of his 60 RBIs won games for the A's. That figure (15 gamers) was the major league high.

The 27-year-old California native enjoyed a nine-game hitting streak from May 29th through June 7th. He also had a five RBI game (vs. Chicago) and a pair of four RBI outings.

The A's one-two combination of leftfielder Rickey Henderson and Murphy absolutely terrifies American League pitchers. It's extremely difficult to get both of them out. (Their 1980 on-base percentage was 41%.) Henderson's .411 on-base percentage and 56 stolen bases account for Murphy's high RBI ratio (hits-to-RBIs).

Defensively, Murphy often plays more like a softball short centerfielder than a standard baseball centerfielder. From his position at "deep shortstop," Murphy often turns bloop hits into outs. But he's quick enough to go get those deep shots, too.

Outfield

TONY ARMAS

OAKLAND A's

Despite a relatively poor season average (only .261), Antonio Rafael Armas Machado was the American League's top rightfielder again in 1981. AL pitchers fear few hitters as much as they fear Tony Armas.

A former Pirate — he came to Oakland from Pittsburgh for the 1977 season — Tony was almost as productive at the plate as he was in 1980 when he hit .279.

He tied Dwight Evans, Bobby Grich, and Eddie Murray for the home run championship (22). He knocked in 76 runs, second to Murray's 78. His 211 total bases was second only to Evans's 215. But for Armas, the best news was that none of those other top sluggers played for a divisional winner.

When the A's got off to their rocket start with 11 straight wins, Tony was at his best. He hit .386 with six homers and 16 RBIs during that streak. Over the first month, Tony had five game-winning and two game-tying RBIs.

Defensively, he's just another one of the speed demons in the Oakland outfield. Armas, however, was the outfield assists' leader.

Tony's unusual hitting style confounds the experts. He lifts his front (right) leg before he swings. "But it's back on the ground before I make contact," says Tony. "Besides, it's your hand position, not your feet that count."

Like some hamburger eaters, A's fans are content to let Tony do it his way.

Catcher

JIM SUNDBERG

TEXAS RANGERS

In a year when American League catchers were the focus of attention, Texas's Jim Sundberg was still the best. Oh, yes, fans of Cleveland's Bo Diaz and Chicago's Carlton Fisk may argue, but Sundberg's day-in and day-out performance behind and at the plate merit him the All-Pro designation.

Almost no one argues about Sundberg's defensive ability. He has been the league's top backstop for half a decade. And Jim does well enough with a bat in his hand to keep him on the top rung of AL receivers.

The 1981 numbers included a .277 batting mark in 102 games. He has never been much in the power department. His 1980 total of 10 homers was his high-water mark. But the .277 average was still 20 points over his career mark.

Jim has spent eight of his nine pro years with the Rangers. He played in 91 games for Double-A Pittsfield, MA, before Texas called for him in 1974. He struggled for a while at bat (hitting .247, .199, and .228) in his first three campaigns before becoming a respectable hitter. He hasn't hit less than .273 since.

One of the things manager Don Zimmer and the Rangers like most about the 30-year-old Sundberg is his durability. He has caught at least 140 games per season (until last year's strike-shortened schedule). Even a 1979 beaning kept him out of the lineup for only a couple of games. (And when he returned, the 6-0, 195-pounder went nine for his next 18 at-bats!)

Pitcher

ROLLIE FINGERS

MILWAUKEE BREWERS

This page is normally reserved for the American League's top right-handed starter. So you'd expect to see the face of Detroit's Jack Morris on the opposite page. But 1981, the year of the strike, was hardly a normal year. So forgive us for honoring the American League's MVP and Cy Young Award winner, Milwaukee's master with moustache, Rollie Fingers.

Rollie got to Milwaukee from San Diego the long way — via St. Louis. The Cards may regret shipping him to Wisconsin without at least taking a look at him.

Fingers was the key to the Brewers' second-half championship. He won the pennant-clincher (a 2-1 win over Detroit), and saved 16 more. Where would the Brewers have been without Fingers? "Probably three games behind Toronto," said manager Buck Rodgers. (The Jays finished last, as usual.)

Some fans were surprised when Fingers added the MVP trophy to his Cy Young award. But not Milwaukee coach Larry Haney. "Nobody in the league did for his team as much as Rollie did for us," he said.

Pressure is the name of the relief pitcher's game. And Rollie thrives on it. The only four-time winner of the Fireman of the Year Award, Fingers loves his job. "The day I stop enjoying it, that's the day I'll quit."

At age 35, that doesn't figure to be soon. And with the all-time major-league saves record already in his pocket, Rollie may be on the way to the Hall of Fame.

Pitcher

RON GUIDRY

NEW YORK YANKEES

When the major-league general managers did their pre-Christmas shopping at the free-agent draft last November, the most popular item on their lists was the Yankees' ace left-hander, Ron Guidry.

Eighteen of the 21 clubs eligible to draft Guidry (including the Yanks) tabbed the fireballing lefty during the Nov. 13th session. As a result, the phone in the office of Guidry's lawyer-agent John Schneider never stopped ringing. Some of the callers were turned off by Ron's million-dollars-plus per year demands. But many of them vowed to stay in the hunt until they had Guidry's name on a contract.

Ron's 1981 season wasn't all fun and games. Hampered by a bone bruise on the ball of his right foot in May, Guidry struggled. He was 5-3 with a 3.74 ERA when the players took a hike in early June.

The second half was more vintage Guidry. He won his first six decisions and was named the AL's Pitcher of the Month for August. Despite a broken finger on his non-throwing hand, he wound up 11-5 with a 2.76 ERA. Over the last four seasons, Guidry has won 82 games, second only to the Phillie's Steve Carlton (84), among big leaguers.

The big question on the minds of those trying to sign Guidry last winter: Is he a complete game pitcher? Ron failed to finish any of the 21 games he started in '81. That's okay when you have Goose Gossage mopping up for you. But most teams aren't that lucky.

Dusty Baker — LA Dodgers

National League All-Pro Team 1981

1B: Pete Rose
2B: Manny Trillo
3B: Mike Schmidt
SS: Dave Concepcion
OF: George Foster
OF: Andre Dawson
OF: Dusty Baker
C: Gary Carter
RHP: Tom Seaver
LHP: Fernando Valenzuela

First Base

PETE ROSE

PHILADELPHIA PHILLIES

That Pete Rose is headed for baseball's Hall of Fame is not a question. The question is when. A player must be retired for five years to qualify, and there's no reason to believe that Rose is thinking much about retirement. And why should he?

At age 41, he is coming off one of his finest seasons ever. He hit .325, second in the NL, and led the league in hits (140) for the seventh time, an NL record.

When Pete is ready to call it a career, chances are he'll need his own section in the record book. He became the National League's all-time hit leader last August 10. His 3,631st hit put him ahead of the immortal Stan Musial. The next target: Ty Cobb's major-league hit record (4,191). Pete needs another 494 hits to catch Cobb.

Rose leaves nothing to chance. His long career is the reward for taking great care of his body. And he's a thinking man's player. Late in a game, he'll switch to a lighter bat ("a half-ounce makes a big difference," says Rose). He wipes his bats clean before every game. ("The marks on the bat tell me what I'm doing up there," he says.)

When Phillie owner Ruly Carpenter gave 38-year-old Pete a four-year contract, the fans thought he was crazy. As it turns out, Carpenter is gone (he sold the club last winter) and Rose is still there, doing an all-star job. He hasn't missed a single game since coming to Philly. There's no telling how long he may stay!

Third Base

MIKE SCHMIDT

PHILADELPHIA PHILLIES

Talk about your solid baseball citizens. Mike Schmidt could be elected mayor of Philadelphia — if he wanted it. The guy just does a super job, day in and day out, season after season. With his second straight National League MVP Award locked firmly away, the Phillie third baseman is looking for new worlds to conquer at age 32.

The 6-2, 203-pound Schmidt does everything and does it well. At bat and in the field, nobody does it better. A certified slugger, Mike swatted 31 homers in '81 to lead the majors in four-baggers for the fifth time in nine years. His total of 31 was good for a full season for most mortals. Mike accomplished it in only 102 games. His 310th homer, off Pittsburgh's Kent Tekulve last September 20th, set an all-time mark for a Philadelphia player. (The old record holder: Hall of Famer Jimmy Foxx.)

If anything, 1981 was Mike's best year at the plate. He led the NL in homers, of course. But he was also the slugging leader (.644) for the third straight year, the runs-scored leader (78), the walks leader (73), the RBI leader (91) for the second straight year, and the on-base percentage leader (.435).

Put that all together with the best hot-corner glove in the league and you have an All-Star for all seasons.

Second Base

MANNY TRILLO

PHILADELPHIA PHILLIES

Manny Trillo could easily be called "The Unknown Soldier" of Philadelphia. It's hard to make noise when your teammates include all-timer Pete Rose, two-time MVP Mike Schmidt, and super-pitcher "Lefty" Carlton.

So the 31-year-old Trillo (his birthday falls on Christmas Day) just goes out quietly and plays the best second base in the National League. And he does it at the plate and in the field.

A past Gold Glove winner, Manny shores up the Phillies's middle defense. The 6-1, 164-pounder from Venezuela doesn't pack much heft onto his wiry frame. But he makes up for it with great bat control and super baseball sense. His .287 batting average in the shortened '81 season was second only to his .292 performance for the world champion 1980 Phillies.

Manny came to Philadelphia from the Cubs just before the '79 season. He suffered a broken arm (hit by a Rick Sutcliffe fastball) and missed 40 games that season. But since then, Trillo has been healthy and successful.

Trillo fans will remember that their man is the answer to a baseball trivia question. When Oakland owner Charlie Finley tried to replace second baseman Mike Andrews during the 1973 World Series, rookie Manny Trillo was the man he picked. Commissioner Bowie Kuhn nixed the roster change and Trillo had to wait until 1980 and Philly to play in a World Series.

Shortstop

DAVE CONCEPCION

CINCINNATI REDS

Agent Jerry Kapstein turns out to be a Cincinnati hero. Kapstein is Dave Concepcion's negotiator. Before Concepcion could go through the free-agent process last winter, the agent and the shortstop signed a Reds contract, which should keep Davey in Cincinnati for the rest of his career.

The reported numbers are five years at approximately $926,000 per year. That's nearly five times as much as Concepcion earned under his old $200,000 per year contract. Dave will not starve, but more important to Reds' fans, he'll be eating in Cincinnati.

By the time his new contract expires, Dave will be 39 years old. And if he plays as well as he has during the past five years, the Reds may want to sign him to another contract.

Davey has always been known for his ability in the field. But 1981 also marked Concepcion's best year at the plate. His .306 batting average was 37 points higher than his career mark, and five better than his previous high. And he became Cincinnati's Mr. Clutch, drilling 14 game-winning RBI hits, the league's best total.

The 6-1, 180-pound Venezuelan has always hit well in the clutch. Since 1973, when a broken ankle cost him half a season, he has had only one season with fewer than 60 RBIs, including 67 in the short '81 campaign.

Outfield

GEORGE FOSTER

CINCINNATI REDS

You remember Frank Duffy and Vern Geishert, of course. You don't? They're the players the Reds sent to San Francisco in exchange for George Foster back in 1971. Under "one-sided trades" in the dictionary, you'll find this classic.

Teammate Ray Knight has been watching George tear up National League pitching for a couple of years. He says it all: "George is the most destructive hitter in baseball. When he's hot, he can tear up a team singlehandedly."

It was another routinely super year for the 33-year-old in 1981. He hit .295, 22 points over his lifetime average. His 90 RBIs placed him second in the NL behind Philly's Mike Schmidt (91). But over the last six seasons, no one has more RBIs than the man with the big black bat. George's 671 total gives him a hefty edge on Jim Rice, Steve Garvey, and Schmidt.

When it comes to hitting in the clutch, Cincinnati usually turns to Foster. His total of 13 game-winning RBIs was second on the team (and in the league) to Dave Concepcion's 14. Foster also ranked among the league leaders in slugging percentage (third at .519), runs scored (seventh with 64), hits (sixth with 122), and on-base percentage (ninth at .373).

Foster's 1982 ambition? To right the wrong of '81 when the Reds, with baseball's best record, failed to qualify for post-season play. A world title would do it for George.

Outfield

ANDRE DAWSON

MONTREAL EXPOS

San Diego manager Dick Williams doesn't look forward to visiting Montreal this season. Not only must he face the Eastern champion Expos, his old team, but he must take on the man he called "the National League's best all-around player."

That's Andre Dawson, the Expos's outstanding centerfielder. According to Williams, Andre has no weaknesses. His season batting average was .302. And he hits with power as his 24 homers (second in the NL) clearly prove.

"His speed speaks for itself," says Williams. "It allows him to play a shallow centerfield. You can't get a bloop hit against him. And nobody goes back on the ball any better. His arm was always good and he has learned, with lots of practice, to release the ball quickly."

But what Williams and the Expos's new manager, Jim Fanning, love most about Dawson is his attitude. "He's one of the most unselfish players I've seen," says Fanning.

"He tends to be quiet," says Williams. "But he's a leader on the club. He never raises his voice, but when he talks, everyone listens."

If the Expos intend to repeat as the NL East's top dog, their centerfielder must lead them.

Outfield

DUSTY BAKER

LOS ANGELES DODGERS

The world-champion Dodgers had lots of heroes. Fernando Valenzuela captured most of the 1981 headlines. First baseman Steve Garvey is always in the news. And catcher Steve Yeager was a surprise World Series hero.

But the guy who does his job best may be the quiet man in left field — Dusty Baker. Nineteen eighty-one may have been his best year ever. His .320 batting mark was the Dodgers's best and third in the NL. He also was the LA hit leader with 128 (fourth in the league). He was rewarded with his first All-Star Game shot. More should follow.

At age 32, Dusty has really found a home with the Dodgers. A one-time all-sports star in Riverside, CA, Baker was solid all year long. He set a 1981 Dodger high by hitting in 15 straight games — with a two-month break for the strike.

It's hard to believe, but Dusty was a 26th round draft choice by the Braves back in 1967. By the 26th round, most teams are down to picking batboys and team mascots. But the scouts were turned off by Dusty's practice of running in track meets the same day as baseball games.

With a $4-million contract that should keep him in the Dodger outfield through 1985, at least, Dusty has found happiness. "I'm in my prime now," he says. "I'm feeling good. And we've got a great ballclub." Who could ask for anything more?

Catcher

GARY CARTER

MONTREAL EXPOS

The No. 1 *receveur* in the National League? No question, it's Gary Carter of the Montreal Expos. *Receveur* is the French equivalent of catcher, and in either language, Carter has put considerable distance between himself and the rest of the NL backstops.

The 6-2, 215-pounder showed his best stuff during the final weeks of the '81 season. As the Expos drove toward their first-ever post-season play, Carter hobbled around on torn ankle ligaments. Without a first-rate back-up, manager Jim Fanning had to keep Gary in the lineup. Carter never let his manager or his teammates down.

The Eastern title capped another wonderful year for the 28-year-old Carter. He won his first All-Star Game starting berth and responded by winning the MVP trophy. For the season, he hit only .251, but knocked in a team-high 68 runs (fourth in the NL), battered 16 homers (seventh in the league), and had seven of the Expos's 56 game-winning RBIs.

Montreal fans agree that Gary is almost too good to be true. A three-sport star in high school in Fullerton, CA, Gary turned down numerous college scholarship offers to sign with the Expos organization in 1972. He was also a stickout in the classroom, finishing in the top 50 in his graduating class and being named to the National Honor Society.

Pitcher

TOM SEAVER

CINCINNATI REDS

Reasonably, a baseball fan must be at least 20 years old to remember when Tom Seaver was *not* the best right-handed pitcher in the National League, much less the major leagues.

Tom Terrific has been doing it for the Mets and then the Reds since 1967. Sure, there have been some good years sprinkled among the great. And folks start talking about how Seaver is reaching the end. And then Tom turns around and has a year like he had in '81, and the talk stops.

Tom's 14-2 record, baseball's best percentage, led the Reds to the best overall record in the National League's 1981 seasons. At age 37, he has done it all. His next target: the magic 300-win circle. He needs 41 more victories, and it would be foolish to believe that he won't make it.

Seaver is a true student of his art. He knows pitching inside out, and practices what he knows to perfection. His scientific explanations sometimes turn off his critics. They can't understand how a variation in rhythm can turn a star into a bum on a given day. Still, Seaver goes out and shows them just how his next time out.

When Tom finally decides to hang it up, he'll have a choice of his future activities. A proven success as a broadcaster, he has all the makings of a great big-league manager. Whatever he chooses, he'll do superbly.

Pitcher

FERNANDO VALENZUELA

LOS ANGELES DODGERS

No doubt about it, 1981 was the year of Fernando. The chunky Dodger left-hander from Mexico even had non-fans bubbling. And why not? Despite a late-season slump,

Fernando pitched more like a grizzled veteran than a young kid.

It all started on opening day. Tom Lasorda had pencilled in Jerry Reuss as his opening day starter. When Reuss came up lame, Lasorda turned to the youngster. And did he ever respond. His five-hit, 2-0 shutout of Houston was the first of *five* whitewashes in the opening month.

When the players' strike put the game into mothballs early in June, Fernando was the talk of the baseball world. TV cameras had already visited Navajoa, his tiny Mexican home town. A book on his 20-year-long life was already available — in both English and Spanish. And since Fernando's English was almost nonexistent, the Dodgers assigned broadcaster Jaime Jarrin to serve as his official translator.

One of the keys to Fernando's success was his potent screwball, taught to him by Dodger reliever Bobby Castillo. That pitch was the main ingredient in a season that saw him rack up eight straight wins at the start of the season, a 36-inning scoreless streak, and eight shutouts — tying the major-league record for a rookie, despite the shortened season. He even batted .250 with seven RBIs. But perhaps the most important number for Fernando, the opponents's .205 batting average against him.

Although Fernando earned only $42,500 last season, chances are he'll pull down a lot more Dodger green in '82.

AMERICAN LEAGUE
STANDINGS OF CLUBS AT CLOSE OF 1981 SEASON
FIRST HALF

WEST

	Won	Lost	Pct.	GB
Oakland	37	23	.617	—
Texas	33	22	.600	1½
Chicago	31	22	.585	2
California	31	29	.517	6
Kansas City	20	30	.400	12½
Seattle	21	36	.368	14
Minnesota	17	39	.304	18

EAST

	Won	Lost	Pct.	GB
New York	34	22	.607	—
Baltimore	31	23	.574	2
Milwaukee	31	25	.554	2½
Detroit	31	26	.544	3
Boston	30	26	.536	4
Cleveland	26	24	.520	5
Toronto	16	42	.276	19

SECOND HALF

	Won	Lost	Pct.	GB
Kansas City	30	23	.566	—
Oakland	27	22	.551	1
Texas	24	26	.480	4½
Minnesota	24	29	.453	6
Seattle	23	29	.442	6½
Chicago	23	30	.434	7
California	20	30	.400	8½

	Won	Lost	Pct.	GB
Milwaukee	31	22	.585	—
Boston	29	23	.558	1½
Detroit	29	23	.558	1½
Baltimore	28	23	.549	2
Cleveland	26	27	.491	5
New York	25	26	.490	5
Toronto	21	27	.438	7½

Rich Gossage

AL East

NEW YORK YANKEES

Better than a good policeman, Yankee owner George Steinbrenner always gets his man, and sometimes more than once. With two-time manager Bob Lemon signed for a full go-round in '82, George also announced that Gene Michael would get another shot in '83. But if Bob flops, look for Gene around July 15, 1982.

Bob shouldn't flop. The Yanks always manage to fill their holes with top talent. Ex-Red Ken Griffey (.311) should add punch to the line-up and defense to the outfield. World Series bust Dave Winfield (.294) can be awesome at the plate. C Rick Cerone (.244) is one of the AL's best, though Steinbrenner doesn't believe it at times. Aging Graig Nettles (.244) still owns a vacuum-cleaner glove. Bucky Dent (.238) will have to fight for his job; Larry Milbourne (.313) wants it. 2B Willie Randolph (.232) could be tougher.

The pitching corps was saved when Ron Guidry (11-5, 2.76) signed on again for about a million bucks a year. Tommy John (9-8) continues to amaze, though he's still amazed about his early departure from the last game of the '81 World Series. Yankee starters completed only 16 games last year (Oakland had 60 CGs). But that's OK when Goose Gossage (3-2, 0.77, 20 saves) and Ron Davis (4-5, 2.71) are working behind you.

Gorman Thomas

AL East

MILWAUKEE BREWERS

The '82 Brewers could well be the team that makes Milwaukee famous. The team didn't miss by much last year, taking the Yankees to a fifth game of the pre-playoffs before losing out. The Brewers have hitting, pitching, and defense, and there isn't much more to this kids' game.

Few players enjoyed a season like 1B Cecil Cooper (.320, 70 runs, 35 doubles). SS Robin Yount, an All-Pro at bat and in the field, hit .273 and provided fine leadership. 2B Jim Gantner (.267) appears to have made an outfielder out of Paul Molitor (.267). 3B Roy Howell (.238) and Don Money (.216) are adequate.

Mr. Power, OF Gorman Thomas (.259), missed the home run title by one with 21. Ben Oglivie can do better than last year's .243, but still had 72 RBIs. Mark Brouhard (.274) may see more action this season. C Ted Simmons did for Milwaukee what he did for St. Louis in the past. He produced 12 game-winning RBIs.

Cy Young Award winner Rollie Fingers (6-3, 1.04, 28 saves) was a key to Milwaukee's success. Brewer pitchers, despite a poor 3.91 team ERA, were more effective knowing that Fingers would lend a hand. Pete Vuckovich (14-4, 3.54) tied for the league-lead in wins and had the highest percentage (.778).

Kirk Gibson

AL East

DETROIT TIGERS

If Sparky Anderson doesn't watch out, he's going to find himself in another World Series one of these days. Unlike most of his players, Sparky has been there before (with the Reds). But the young Tigers have the look of a winner.

The 1982 Detroit model has only slight changes, mostly in the outfield. OF Steve Kemp (.277) is gone to Chicago for Chet Lemon (.302). The slugging Kemp was due to become a free agent after this season. So the Tigers shipped him to the Sox for Lemon, who's in a similar position. Another OF pick-up, ex-Giant Larry Herndon, will add strength and power. And Kirk Gibson (.328), the majors' #1 hitter during the second-half of 1981 (.375), is back.

Pitching begins with the AL's top (and winningest) righty starter in '81, Jack Morris (14-7). Righty Milt Wilcox (12-9) seems to have his game together, and reliever Kevin Saucier (4-2, 13 saves — fifth in the league) is solid.

C Lance Parrish (.244) outhit his backup John Wockenfuss (.215) and should remain the starter. SS Alan Trammell (.258) and 1B Lou Whitaker (.263) are capable. 3B-DH Richie Hebner can do better than .226.

Eddie Murray

AL East

BALTIMORE ORIOLES

Earl Weaver is beginning to make strange noises in Baltimore. It sounds like he's ready to retire, but he'd surely like another American League pennant first.

He might just have the talent to do it. The 1981 Birds went 59-46, just one game behind Milwaukee in the overall East standings. The three former Cy Young award winners Steve Stone (tendinitis), Mike Flanagan (torn forearm muscles), and Jim Palmer (shoulder and neck), went 4-7, 9-6, and 7-8 respectively. But Tippy Martinez (3-3) had 11 saves and Dennis Martinez (14-5) and Scott McGregor (13-5) were outstanding. SS Mark Belanger took his .165 batting average to Los Angeles. But the O's are still set with 1B Eddie Murray (.294, but .387 hitting right-handed), 3B Doug DeCinces (.263), and 2B Rich Dauer (.263). Look for a new shortstop, perhaps Cal Ripken (.128 in 23 games).

Al Bumbry (.273) and Ken Singleton, due to bounce back, are the key outfielders. C Rick Dempsey (.215) may become a switch-hitter.

Carney Lansford

AL East

BOSTON RED SOX

Off a surprisingly good 59-49 season, Red Sox manager Ralph Houk has a new contract and high hopes. And why not? The Sox could always hit and there seem to be a few live arms on the pitching staff as well.

The former California Angels in the Red Sox infield enjoyed a super 1981. 3B Carney Lansford, often referred to as the Unknown Batting Champion, led the league with .336. 2B Jerry Remy was consistently at the .300 mark, finishing at .307.

1B-DH Tony Perez slumped to .252 with only 39 RBIs. But OFs Jim Rice (.284 and 62 RBI) and Dwight Evans (.296, 22 homers, 71 RBIs) more than picked up the slack. Carl Yastrzemski, at age 42, should have another year left.

Righty Mike Torrez led the pitchers with a 10-3 mark though his ERA (3.68) was relatively high. Bob Stanley (10-8) and Dennis Eckersley (9-8) are proven pros, and ex-Angel Mark Clear (8-3) was a pleasant surprise. Righty Luis Aponte (1-0, 0.57 in seven late season relief jobs) should help the bullpen. The Sox also expect big things from SS Julio Valdez and utility men Chico Walker and Wade Boggs.

AL East

CLEVELAND INDIANS

Mike Hargrove

With the Indians, it's simply a case of being in the wrong place at the wrong time. The 1981 team went 52-51 and finished sixth and fifth in the two halves of the tough East pennant race.

No fewer than seven of the 1981 Indians are gone, including vets like Jorge Orta (.272), Bo Diaz (.313), and Duane Kuiper (.257). In an effort to improve its ragged pitching, Cleveland added at least four new pitchers to the roster, led by ex-Cards Silvio Martinez and Lary Sorenson, ex-Dodger Rick Sutcliffe, and ex-Giant Ed Whitson. Sorenson and Whitson should be in the starting rotation with righties Len "Perfect Game" Barker (8-7) and Bert Blyleven (11-7, 2.88).

C Ron Hassey (.232) should replace Diaz, with help from Chris Bando (.306 at Charleston). 1B Mike Hargrove (.317, 49 RBIs) is solid. Ex-Dodger Jack Perconte may fit in. 3B Toby Harrah (.291) comes off another fine season. Tom Veryzer (.244) is now a New York Met.

OF Miguel Dilone (.290) continues to surprise. A comeback by Joe Charboneau (.210) is a key to Cleveland's success. Rick Manning can do better than last year's .244.

John Mayberry

AL East

TORONTO BLUE JAYS

Things are still tough in Toronto. The Jays won only 37 of 106 games last year and finished last in both halves of the East pennant chase. Despite a new manager, ex-Brave boss Bobby Cox, 1982 may be no better. The best thing in Toronto is the marvelous support provided by the Jay fans in the face of poor performance.

It's hard to build a club without good players and it's hard to get good players without other good players to trade. The Jays have little of either. Everyone wants P Dave Stieb (11-10), Toronto's winningest pitcher. But they're apparently offering very little. Righty Joey McLaughlin went 1-5 but had 10 saves.

IFs Damaso Garcia and Alfredo Griffin are adequate, but their .252 and .209 batting averages just aren't good enough. 1B-DH John Mayberry is solid (.248, 17 homers) but can't do it on defense. Aging (34) Aurelio Rodriquez joins Toronto (from the Yanks) with a part-time .346 mark last year playing behind 3B Graig Nettles. He could help.

Among the outfielders, Al Woods' .247 average was tops — and that says it all. Lloyd Moseby (.233), Barry Bonnell (.220), and George Bell (.233) must improve at bat. Watch for Mitch Webster (.294 at Knoxville).

Willie Wilson

AL West

KANSAS CITY ROYALS

Despite a second-half mini-pennant — and a shot at the 1981 playoffs, the Royals were a major disappointment last season. They should be back in the hunt this year. There's just too much talent in Kaycee to write this team off.

Manager Dick Howser, starting his first full season in Missouri, has the same basic cast, save for the departure of the once-heralded OF Clint Hurdle (.329 in only 28 games). P Scott Brown arrived from Cincinnati in exchange for Hurdle.

Righty Dennis Leonard (13-11) and lefty Larry Gura (11-8) head the mound crew. Both had ERAs under 3.00. Lefty Paul Splittorff was under-par at 5-5, 4.36. Righty Dan Quisenberry (1-4, 18 saves) may get bullpen help from Splittorff.

Jamie Quirk (.250) and John Wathan (.252) were adequate behind the plate. 3B George Brett let everyone down by batting "only" .314, but it was a struggle. 2B Frank White (.250) is the AL's top glove-man at second. Tiny (5-6) Onix Concepcion (.256 at Omaha) may find a spot. 1B Willie Aikens (.266) again displayed good power.

The outfield is okay with rangy Amos Otis (.269) and speedy Willie Wilson (.303, 34 steals). There are questions about OF-DH Hal McRae (.272).

Steve McCatty

AL West

OAKLAND A's

Billyball is back, and Oakland has it. Baseball's #1 surprise team of '81 will sneak up on no one in '82. Still, Billy Martin's A's still figure to be in the thick of things all year long.

And why not? Oakland owns the absolutely finest outfield in the world. Rickey Henderson (.319), Dwayne Murphy (.251), and Tony Armas (.261), All-Pros all, can hit, hit with power, and run. And no one has ever seen a quicker set of outfielders.

The infield may be the Oakland downfall. In fact, though the outfielders averaged 108 games each, none of the infielders got into more than 84. You can't put folks like 3B Wayne Gross (.206), steady-fielding SS Rob Piccolo (.268), 2B Dave McKay (.263), 1B Jim Spencer (.188), Fred Stanley (.193), and the rest in the same class. Catcher Mike Heath (.236) is adequate defensively.

But there's nothing like Oakland's starting pitchers. Though finishing second to the Yankees in ERA (2.90 to 3.30), the A's moundsmen still led the AL with 60 complete games (no one else had more than 33). If there's a weakness, it's that the starting four are all righties: Mike Norris (12-9, 3.75), Steve McCatty (14-7, 2.33), Rick Langford (12-10, 2.99), and Matt Keough (10-6, 3.40).

Al Oliver

AL West
TEXAS RANGERS

The Rangers have been knocking on the AL West door for so long, they must have sore knuckles. Only Oakland did better than Texas (57-48 overall) a year ago. And the potential for a division title is there.

Manager Don Zimmer has a bunch of legitimate stars in his line-up. C Jim Sundberg (.277) is the AL's best. So is 3B Bobby Bell (.294). OFs Al Oliver and Mickey Rivers are 35 and 33 years old, respectively, but they can still do the job. Oliver hit .309 (eighth in the AL) in '81; Rivers hit .286. The rest of the outfield cast, including Leon Roberts (.279) and Billy Sample (.283), isn't too shabby. The Rangers hit .270 overall in '81, third best in the league. But Zimmer and GM Eddie Robinson were still looking for a right-handed power-hitting outfielder during the off-season.

Ranger pitching was among the best, too. The team ERA (3.40) trailed only the Yanks and A's. Fergie Jenkins (5-8) is gone, but lefty Rick Honeycutt (11-6, 3.31) and righty Doc Medich (10-6, 3.08) are back. Righty John Butcher (1-2 with a 1.63 ERA in a late-season trial) should fit in. So should lefty reliever Mark Mercer (10-8 at Wichita). The American Association's leading hitter, 2B Mike Richardt (.354 at Wichita) could be a starter.

Ken Forsch

AL West

CALIFORNIA ANGELS

Does any of this make sense? Don Baylor's 1981 batting average was .239. Fred Lynn's 1981 batting average was .219. Juan Beniquez's 1981 batting average was .181. Even Rod Carew hit like a human in 1981, an un-Carewlike .305. Put 'em all together, they spell last place, which is where the Angels finished in the second-half race last summer.

The Angels simply aren't a last-place club. There's just too much talent there. The middle of the infield is the AL's best, with SS Rick Burleson (.293) and 2B Bobby Grich (.304, 22 homers). Both are All-Pros. 3B Butch Hobson (.235) is a problem.

The Angels may have to make room for OF Tom Brunansky (.332 at Salt Lake City). Dan Ford (.277) is steady. C Brian Downing (.249) is a former AL All-Star. He'll be pushed by ex-Phillie Bob Boone, purchased by the Angels in December.

California pitching was just average in '81 and may not get much better. A pair of greybeards, 35-year-old Ken Forsch (11-7, 2.88) and 37-year-old Steve Renko (8-4, 3.44) were the big '81 winners. Righty Don Aase (4-4, 2.34) had 11 saves. Lefty Geoff Zahn (10-11) can improve. Look for lefty Mickey Mahler (10-4 at Salt Lake City) to help the mound staff.

Bill Almon

AL West

CHICAGO WHITE SOX

A pair of genuine superstars, pitcher Don Drysdale and 1B Ken Harrelson, will be with the Sox in 1982. Unfortunately, they'll be in the TV booth. The Chicagoans could use some players of their rank on the field.

But the Sox look like they have some punch to join their fine pitchers and make a run in the West. Ex-Tiger Steve Kemp joins slugging Greg Luzinski (.265, 21 homers) and C Carlton Fisk (.263, 45 RBIs). Ex-Mariner Tom Paciorek (.326) cost Chicago three players, but he's worth it! Speedy Ron LeFlore (.246, 36 steals) may get help from Leo Sutherland (.273, 50 steals at Edmonton). Surprising SS Bill Almon (.301) will have to prove that '81 was no fluke. Lamar Johnson (.276) is expected back. And 1B Mike Squires (.265) can improve. 2B Jay Loviglio (.298 at Edmonton) may find a spot.

Pitching is solid. Lefty Britt Burns turned in a solid 10-6 performance. Steve Trout can improve on his 8-7 mark. Ed Farmer (3-3) and Lamarr Hoyt (9-3) each had 10 saves. Righty Reggie Patterson was 10-8 at Edmonton.

Richie Zisk

AL West

SEATTLE MARINERS

The M's couldn't win with Tom Paciorek and Dan Meyer. So now they'll try to win without them. OF Paciorek and OF-3B Meyer were key players in two big off-season deals.

Paciorek (.326), the team's MVP and best hitter ever, goes to the White Sox for three young players who could help this team: C Jim Essian (.308 in only 27 games), SS Todd Cruz, and OF Rod Allen. Meyer was dealt to Oakland for pitching prospect Rich Bordi.

Elsewhere, Seattle isn't exactly without talent. The sixth-place (overall) club in the AL West features the AL's #1 designated hitter, Richie Zisk (.311, including a 15-game hit streak). 2B Julio Cruz (.256) stole 32 straight bases, tying an AL mark. OF Jeff Burroughs (.254, 10 homers) is a powerhouse when healthy. 1B Bruce Bochte (.260) bounced back from a .179 April. Versatile Len Randle (.267) played six positions and seems to be going the right way.

New catcher Essian will handle a so-so mound staff, headed by all-time Mariner win leader, righty Glenn Abbott (4-9 after an 0-4 start). Righty Larry Andersen (3-3) is the most consistent reliever. Lefty Floyd Bannister was 9-9, his best season yet.

Doug Corbett

AL West

MINNESOTA TWINS

Despite a mild rally which took them to fourth-place in the second-half AL West race in '81, the Twins still had the division's worst overall record. But that was outdoors. The '82 Twins will never see the light of day — at least not at home.

The new 54,000-seat Hubert H. Humphrey Metrodome will protect the Twins from the sun, wind, rain, and, late in the season, maybe snow. But the dome won't protect the players from themselves, and that's manager Billy Gardner's problem.

The Twins have little to write home about. Catcher Butch Wynegar, a one-time AL All-Star, missed half a season and hit only .247. Sal Butera finished the job but hit only .240. 3B John Castino can do better than his .268. And neither Rob Wilfong (.246) nor Pete Mackanin (.231) is the answer in anyone's dreams. SS Roy Smalley (.263) is a thorough professional.

Ex-Dodger Mickey Hatcher is a sparkplug, despite his .255 plate record. Hosken Powell (.239) can do better. There's OF hope from Randy Bush (.290, 22 homers at Orlando) and long-range hope from Randy Johnson (.255, 32 homers at Glens Falls). Pitching is spotty. Reliever Doug Corbett (2-6 but 17 saves) is a stickout.

NATIONAL LEAGUE
STANDINGS OF CLUBS AT CLOSE OF 1981 SEASON
FIRST HALF

EAST

	Won	Lost	Pct.	GB
Phildelphia	34	21	.618	—
St. Louis	30	20	.600	1½
Montreal	30	25	.545	4
Pittsburgh	25	23	.521	5½
New York	17	34	.333	15
Chicago	15	37	.288	17½

WEST

	Won	Lost	Pct.	GB
Los Angeles	36	21	.632	—
Cincinnati	35	21	.625	½
Houston	28	29	.491	8
Atlanta	25	29	.463	9½
San Francisco	27	32	.458	10
San Diego	23	33	.411	12½

SECOND HALF

	Won	Lost	Pct.	GB
Montreal	30	23	.566	—
St. Louis	29	23	.558	½
Philadelphia	25	27	.481	4½
New York	24	28	.462	5½
Chicago	23	28	.451	6
Pittsburgh	21	33	.389	9½

	Won	Lost	Pct.	GB
Houston	33	20	.623	—
Cincinnati	31	21	.596	1½
San Francisco	29	23	.558	3½
Los Angeles	27	26	.509	6
Atlanta	25	27	.481	7½
San Diego	18	36	.333	15½

Steve Carlton

NL East

PHILADELPHIA PHILLIES

Pat Corrales never had it so good. When Phillie field boss Dallas Green moved to Chicago this winter, the one-time Ranger manager took over. And he never had talent like this in Texas.

Corrales' arrival is part of a total front-office changeover. Long-time owner Ruly Carpenter bailed out after the '81 season, selling the club ($30 million) to a group headed by Phillie exec Bill Giles.

But games are won on the field, by the likes of All-Pros like ageless 1B Pete Rose (.325, second in the NL), All-World 3B Mike Schmidt (.316, 31 homers, 91 RBIs, 78 runs), and 2B Manny Trillo (.287).

Pitcher Steve "Lefty" Carlton (13-4, 2.42 ERA) would have been the NL's top portsider in any year except the Year of Fernando. But Phillie pitchers suffered with the NL's worst team ERA in '81 (4.05) which presents Corrales' biggest problem. Ex-Cub Mike Krukow (9-9, 3.69 ERA) might help.

One major addition is ex-Indian C Bo Diaz (.313) who brings top credentials to Philly. His arrival allowed Giles to dump long-time Phillie Bob Boone (.211) and young Keith Moreland (.255). There will be more new faces in Philly by opening day.

Steve Rogers

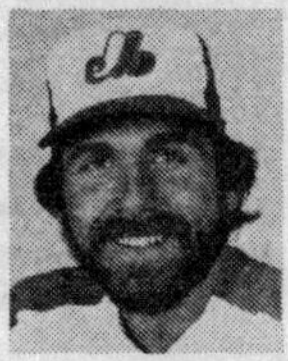

NL East

MONTREAL EXPOS

You have to love the Expos' fans. When they're happy, they sing. And there should be plenty of choruses of "Valderi, Valdera" throughout the 1982 season.

Manager Jim Fanning, starting his first full season, has solid players at most positions. C Gary Carter (.251, 68 RBIs) is the class of the National League. OF Andre Dawson (.302), only 27, should be an All-Star straight through to 1990. And speedy Tim Raines (.304, 71 steals in only 88 games) may threaten all of Lou Brock's stolen-base marks.

Pitching could be a problem, but righty Steve Rogers (12-8, 3.41) is solid, as is righty Scott Sanderson (9-7, 2.96). Ex-Met Jeff Reardon (3-0, 2.19, 8 saves) is a top bullpen operator and may get help from lefty Tom Gorman (12-9, 20 saves at Memphis).

There's additional speed, power, and defense, with 2B Rodney Scott (.205 and a fine glove), 1B Warren Cromartie (.304), and 3B Larry Parrish (.244). Ex-Met Frank Taveras could fit in anywhere.

If there's a rookie manager with a better chance to go to a World Series than the 54-year-old Fanning, we don't know who it is.

Keith Hernandez

NL East

ST. LOUIS CARDINALS

It's hard to make lasting friendships in Whitey Herzog's St. Louis. The majors top wheeler-dealer was nearly as active this winter as he was last year. And since St. Louis had the best overall record in the NL East last year (59-43 and second in both halves of the pennant race), Whitey seems to know what he's doing.

Ex-Phillie speedster Lonnie Smith (.324) is the newest Cardinal, which doesn't thrill Phillie fans — unless the pitchers St. Louis gave up do the job in Philly. OF Sixto Lezcano is an ex-Cardinal (.266), and he's not unhappy in San Diego. Pitcher Steve Mura (5-14) came to St. Louis in the deal, with players like Card Garry Templeton (.288 but a bomb with St. Loo fans) and Padre Ozzie Smith (.222) expected to be thrown into the deal.

The Cards should be in the thick of the NL East race, with Gold Glove 1B Keith Hernandez (.306 but lousy against lefties) one of the game's premier hitters. Look for Keith to spend some time in the outfield this time around. OF George Hendrick (.284) is moody but a pro. So is Ken Oberkfell (.293). C Darrell Porter (.224) and Gene Tenace (.233) may be ready to give way to Orlando Sanchez (.286).

Righty Bruce Sutter (3-5, 25 saves) heads a strong bullpen.

Bill Madlock

NL East

PITTSBURGH PIRATES

By opening day, you may not recognize the Pirates — except for their gold uniforms. A last-place finish in the second-half pennant race prompted Pittsburgh management to talk about cleaning house. And it may just happen.

The main moving candidate was giant OF Dave Parker (.258, only nine homers). Dave suffered from both overweight and an Achilles tendon problem in missing 35 Buc games in '81. Hot 1B prospect Doe Boyland (.310 at Portland) went to San Francisco for P Tom Griffin (8-8) during the off-season.

NL bat champ Bill Madlock (.341) should be back, but SS Tim Foli (.247) is gone to California for C Brian Harper. That increases IF Vance Law's chances for making the major-league roster. Dale Berra had an adequate season (.241 in 81 games). 1B Jason Thompson (.242, 15 homers) was a disappointment.

The Buc outfield is anchored by now-steady Mike Easler (.286) and flashy Omar Moreno (.276). But catching could be a problem if second-year man Tony Pena (.300 in 66 games) can't do the job. Pirate pitching was adequate (a 3.56 ERA). Righty Robert Long (15-3 at Portland) could really help.

Bill Buckner

NL East

CHICAGO CUBS

The Cubs, the team with the worst record (38-65) in the NL last year, may not be any better in '82. But it won't be for lack of effort.

The team's new owners, the Chicago Tribune, swept the house clean, bringing in ex-Phillie manager, Dallas Green, as front-office boss. Green brought in his old coach, Lee Elia, as manager, and proceeded to look for new faces.

Ex-Giant righty Allen Ripley was 4-4 in San Fran; ex-Ranger Fergie Jenkins has won 264 games lifetime. Ex-Phillie catcher Keith Moreland (.255) may be the best of the new pick-ups. But ex-Red Junior Kennedy (.250) could win a spot at second. Ex-Red Sox free agent Bill Campbell could provide relief help if he's sound. And ex-Phils Dicky Noles (2-2) and Dan Larson (3-0) may help too.

OF Leon Durham (.290) is as close as any Cub to being an untouchable. But 1B Bill Buckner (.311) is one of baseball's soundest hitters.

Ellis Valentine

NL East

NEW YORK METS

Last time George Bamberger wore a manager's uniform he had the Milwaukee Brewers in a pennant race. Chances are he won't be in that situation with his new employers, the New York Mets.

The Mets won only 41 of 103 games under Joe Torre in 1981. Only Chicago fared worse in the NL East, and the Cubs seem improved.

The Mets dumped their double-play combination — SS Frank Taveras (.230) and former Gold Glove 2B Doug Flynn (.222). Taveras brought Expos' minor league P Steve Ratzer. Flynn (and P Dan Boitano) brought Texas reliever Jim Kern (1-2) who was hurting for most of '81. That leaves young Ron Gardenhire (.271) and Wally Backman (.278) to fill the middle in '82. Backman suffered with numerous physical and mental problems last year.

The Mets have some solid pros, including reliever Neil Allen (7-6, 18 saves), C John Stearns (.271), and perhaps the club's best-ever third baseman in second-year-man Hubie Brooks (.307). But OF Joel Youngblood (.350 in 43 games) may be gone by opening day, Rusty Staub (.317) is nearing the end of his career, and slugger Dave Kingman (.221, 22 homers) must be more consistent.

Johnny Bench

NL West

CINCINNATI REDS

The Reds got great news during the off-season. Commissioner Bowie Kuhn announced that there would be no split-season in 1982. And Cincinnati loved it. The Reds went 66-42 — the majors' best in '81 — and had nothing to show for it.

It could be different in '82. Though Ken Griffey (.311) has moved on to the Yankees, the Reds are solid all around. Ex-Royal Clint Hurdle (.329 in only 29 KC games) may be able to fill the gap. But rookies Paul Householder (.300 at Indianapolis) and Eddie Milner (.287 at Indianapolis) will also try to make the Cincy outfield.

P Tom Seaver, off a sparkling 14-2 season, is still the key to the Red mound staff at age 37. Righty Mario Soto (12-9) had a super season with 10 complete games (second in the NL), 151 strikeouts, and 175 innings. Ex-Yank farmhand Brian Ryder may help.

Veteran OF George Foster (.295) is still one of baseball's most productive hitters. At age 33, SS Dave Concepcion (.306) has never been better. Cincy signed him for five more years during the winter.

Joe Nolan (.309) is ready to become the Reds' regular catcher, with Johnny Bench (.309 in 52 games) no longer able to do it day in and day out.

Nolan Ryan

NL West

HOUSTON ASTROS

Pitchers love to work in Houston. Whether it's the lighting in the Astrodome, the air, or even the far-out fences, baseballs have a tendency to stay in the field of play. It's a pitcher's paradise.

Houston won the NL team ERA title by about seven miles in '81 (2.66 to second-place LA's 3.01). And why not? Nolan Ryan (11-5) parlayed his record fifth no-hitter into a 1.69 ERA, the league's best. He beat out teammate Bob Knepper (9-5, 2.18). The Astros are concerned about ace Don Sutton (11-9, 2.60), felled by a broken kneecap (on a Jerry Reuss pitch).

IF Art Howe blossomed in '81 with a .296 average and a club-record 23-game hit streak. SS Craig Reynolds (.260) is polished and 1B Cesar Cedeno (.271) is still capable of great things.

C Alan Ashby (.271) manages his pitchers well with help from Luis Pujols (.239). Rookie Alan Knicely (.306 at Tucson) could win a spot. There's not much punch from the outfield — Jose Cruz (.267), Terry Puhl (.251), Gary Woods (.209), and Tony Scott (.293). Rookie Scott Loucks (.271 at Tucson) may fit in.

If you believe in defense and pitching, you've gotta believe in the Astros.

Pedro Guerrero

NL West

LOS ANGELES DODGERS

When the team with the third-best record in the National League wins the world-championship, you begin to believe in Tom Lasorda's theory of the Big Dodger in the Sky. L.A. was pronounced dead at least three times before winning the Series title against the Yanks.

It may be tough for the Dodgers to repeat, but this team has a way of surprising everyone. 1B Steve Garvey (.283, 64 RBIs) overcame personal problems to enjoy a fine season. Minor-league MVP Mike Marshall (.374, 34 homers, 137 RBIs at Albuquerque) is ready to jump in. 3B Ron Cey (.288) overcame a World Series beaning to help the Dodgers win it all. 2B Davey Lopes (.206) and SS Bill Russell (.233) are in trouble, with Steve Sax (.277) and newly-acquired Jorge Orta or Mark Belanger likely to step in.

Pitching is the strong suit, with All-World Fernando Valenzuela (13-7), Jerry Reuss (10-4), and Burt Hooton (11-6) the class of the field.

OFs Dusty Baker (.320) and Pedro Guerrero (.300) are first-rate, with a variety of oldsters and youngsters ready to join them. Mike Scioscia (.276) is the catcher, though Steve Yeager (.209) was a World Series hero.

Chris Chambliss

NL West

ATLANTA BRAVES

New York Met fans will feel right at home in Atlanta Stadium this summer. New manager Joe Torre brought three of his Met coaches — Bob Gibson, Joe Pignatano, and Rube Walker — to Georgia. Fortunately for the New York Four, there seems to be more talent in Atlanta than they had in The Big Apple.

First, there's some honest-to-goodness pitching in Georgia. The team ERA (3.45) was the best in years, with Rick Camp (1.78), Al Hrabosky (1.06), Gene Garber (2.59), and Rick Mahler (2.81) leading the way. There's more in the minors, too, including Joe Cowley, Craig McMurty, Ken Dayley, and Jim Acker. Look for some of the vets to go.

2B Glenn Hubbard (.235) turned in the best fielding ever by a Brave second baseman (.991). 1B Chris Chambliss (.264) is always reliable. And 3B Bob Horner (.277, 15 homers, in 79 games) is super whenever he wants to be.

C Bruce Benedict (.264) made the NL midseason All-Star team and the outfield, with Dale Murphy (.247) and Claudell Washington (.291) is solid. Rookie Brett Butler (.335 at Richmond) should start on opening day.

Jack Clark

NL West

SAN FRANCISCO GIANTS

The Giants claim to be more organized now than they've ever been — at least in the front office. Now if the players can be equally organized, SF has a chance to improve on its 56-55 record.

General manager Tom Haller saw to it that field manager Frank Robinson has a different cast of characters to work with in '82. The newest Giants include a pair of infielders, veteran Duane Kuiper (.257 as an Indian) and 1B-OF prospect Doe Boyland (from the Pirate organization). Both could help. The new moundsmen include ex-Cub Doug Capilla, ex-Tiger Dan Shatzeder, and ex-Royal Rich Gale. The Giants seem to have gotten the better of the deals.

SF hit only .250 as a team last year and could do better if OF Jack Clark (.268), IF Joe Morgan (.240), and Darrell Evans (.258) return to form. C Milt May (.310) and OF Jeff Leonard (.290, but .307 with SF) had super seasons.

P Doyle Alexander (11-7) was the top winner, and Greg Minton (4-5) set a club saves mark with 21. Vida Blue, only 8-6, had a 2.45 ERA. And Al Holland went 7-5 and 2.41.

Terry Kennedy

NL West

SAN DIEGO PADRES

Now it's Dick Williams' turn to try to get the word "disappointing" out of the San Diego vocabulary. You read it every summer: the disappointing San Diego Padres. It has almost become part of the team's name.

But tough guy Williams, who has few friends among the many men who've played for him, might be able to make some progress. He figures to do good things with ex-Brewer and Cardinal OF Sixto Lezcano (.266, but capable of much more). Trade rumors also had super-talent SS Garry Templeton (.288) joining Lezcano in San Diego. (Ozzie Smith, the smooth-fielding SS, would then go on to St. Loo.)

When San Diego traded Rollie Fingers after the '80 season, they hoped that young Gary Lucas could replace him in the bullpen. Lucas responded with 13 saves and 7 wins, for a club that won only 41 games all year. C Terry Kennedy enjoyed his first full big-league season with a .301 bat mark and 24 doubles, sixth in the NL. Rookie 2B Juan Bonilla (.290) was excellent.

Versatile Luis Salazar (.303) and OF Gene Richards (.288 and a league-leading 12 triples) give Williams hope. OF Rupe Jones was second in the NL in doubles (34).

HOW THEY'LL FINISH IN 1982

AMERICAN LEAGUE

East
1. New York Yankees
2. Milwaukee Brewers
3. Detroit Tigers
4. Baltimore Orioles
5. Boston Red Sox
6. Cleveland Indians
7. Toronto Blue Jays

West
1. Kansas City Royals
2. Oakland Athletics
3. Texas Rangers
4. California Angels
5. Chicago White Sox
6. Seattle Mariners
7. Minnesota Twins

NATIONAL LEAGUE

East
1. Philadelphia Phillies
2. Montreal Expos
3. St. Louis Cardinals
4. Pittsburgh Pirates
5. Chicago Cubs
6. New York Mets

West
1. Cincinnati Reds
2. Houston Astros
3. Los Angeles Dodgers
4. Atlanta Braves
5. San Francisco Giants
6. San Diego Padres

American League Champions: New York Yankees
National League Champions: Philadelphia Phillies
World Champs: Phillies

1981

STATISTICS

AMERICAN LEAGUE

Batting

(60 or more at-bats)

***Bats Left-handed †Switch-Hitter**

Batter and Club	AVG	G	AB	R	H	HR	RBI	SB
Adams, Glenn, Minn.*	.209	72	220	13	46	2	24	0
Aikens, Willie, K.C.*	.266	101	349	45	93	17	53	0
Ainge, Danny, Tor	.187	86	246	20	46	0	14	8
Allenson, Gary, Bos	.223	47	139	23	31	5	25	0
Almon, Bill, Chi	.301	103	349	46	105	4	41	16
Anderson, Jim, Sea	.204	70	162	12	33	2	19	3
Armas, Tony, Oak	.261	109	440	51	115	22	76	5
Auerbach, Rick, Sea.	.155	38	84	12	13	1	6	1
Ayala, Benny, Balt	.279	44	86	12	24	3	13	0
Babitt, Shooty, Oak.	.256	54	156	10	40	0	14	5
Baines, Harold, Chi.*	.286	82	280	42	80	10	41	6
Baker, Chuck, Minn	.182	40	66	6	12	0	6	0
Bando, Sal, Milw	.200	32	65	10	13	2	9	1
Bannister, Alan, Clev.	.263	68	232	36	61	1	17	16
Barfield, Jesse, Tor.	.232	25	95	7	22	2	9	4
Baylor, Don, Cal	.239	103	377	52	90	17	66	3
Belanger, Mark, Balt.	.165	64	139	9	23	1	10	2
Bell, Buddy, Tex	.294	97	360	44	106	10	64	3
Bell, George, Tor.	.233	60	163	19	38	5	12	3
Beniquez, Juan, Cal.	.181	58	166	18	30	3	13	2
Bernazard, Tony, Chi.†	.276	106	384	53	106	6	34	4
Bochte, Bruce, Sea.*	.260	99	335	39	87	6	30	1
Bonnell, Barry, Tor	.220	66	227	21	50	4	28	4
Bosetti, Rick, Tor.-Oak.	.197	34	66	9	13	0	5	0
Bosley, Thad, Milw.*	.229	42	105	11	24	0	3	2
Brett, George, K.C.*	.314	89	347	42	109	6	43	14
Brookens, Tom, Det.	.243	71	239	19	58	4	25	5
Brouhard, Mark, Milw.	.274	60	186	19	51	2	20	1
Brown, Bobby, N.Y.†	.226	31	62	5	14	0	6	4
Bulling, Terry, Sea.	.247	62	154	15	38	2	15	0
Bumbry, Al, Balt.*	.273	101	392	61	107	1	27	22
Burleson, Rick, Cal.	.293	109	430	53	126	5	33	4
Burroughs, Jeff, Sea	.254	89	319	32	81	10	41	0
Butera, Sal, Minn.	.240	62	167	13	40	0	18	0

Batter and Club	AVG	G	AB	R	H	HR	RBI	SB
Campaneris, Bert, Cal.	.256	55	82	11	21	1	10	5
Carew, Rod, Cal.*	.305	93	364	57	111	2	21	16
Castino, John, Minn.	.268	101	381	41	102	6	36	4
Cerone, Rick, N.Y.	.244	71	234	23	57	2	21	0
Charboneau, Joe, Clev.	.210	48	138	14	29	4	18	1
Clark, Bobby, Cal.	.250	34	88	12	22	4	19	0
Cooper, Cecil, Milw.*	.320	106	416	70	133	12	60	5
Cowens, Al, Det.	.261	85	253	27	66	1	18	3
Crowley, Terry, Balt.*	.246	68	134	12	33	4	25	0
Cruz, Julio, Sea.†	.256	94	352	57	90	2	24	43
Dauer, Rich. Balt.	.263	96	369	41	97	4	38	0
DeCinces, Doug, Balt.	.263	100	346	49	91	13	55	0
Dempsey, Rick, Balt.	.215	92	251	24	54	6	15	0
Dent, Bucky, N.Y.	.238	73	227	20	54	7	27	0
Diaz, Bo, Clev.	.313	63	182	25	57	7	38	2
Dilone, Miguel, Clev.†	.290	72	269	33	78	0	19	29
Downing, Brian, Cal.	.249	93	317	47	79	9	41	1
Drumright, Keith, Oak.*	.291	31	86	8	25	0	11	0
Dwyer, Jim, Balt.*	.224	68	134	16	30	3	10	0
Edler, Dave, Sea.	.141	29	78	7	11	0	5	3
Engle, Dave, Minn.	.258	82	248	29	64	5	32	0
Evans, Dwight, Bos.	.296	108	412	84	122	22	71	3
Fahey, Bill, Det.*	.254	27	67	5	17	1	9	0
Fisk, Carlton, Chi.	.263	96	338	44	89	7	45	3
Foote, Barry, N.Y.	.208	40	125	12	26	6	10	0
Ford, Dan, Cal.	.277	97	375	53	104	15	48	2
Gamble, Oscar, N.Y.*	.238	80	189	24	45	10	27	0
Gantner, Jim, Milw.*	.267	107	352	35	94	2	33	3
Garcia, Damaso, Tor.	.252	64	250	24	63	1	13	13
Gedman, Rich, Bos.*	.288	62	205	22	59	5	26	0
Geronimo, Cesar, K.C.*	.246	59	118	14	29	2	13	6
Gibson, Kirk, Det.*	.328	83	290	41	95	9	40	17
Goodwin, Danny, Minn.* ..	.225	59	151	18	34	2	17	3
Graham, Dan, Balt.*	.176	55	142	7	25	2	11	0
Gray, Gary, Sea.	.245	69	208	27	51	13	31	2
Grich, Bobby, Cal.	.304	100	352	56	107	22	61	2
Griffin, Alfredo, Tor.†	.209	101	388	30	81	0	21	8
Gross, Wayne, Oak.*	.206	82	243	29	50	10	31	2
Grubb, John, Tex.*	.231	67	199	26	46	3	26	0

Batter and Club	AVG	G	AB	R	H	HR	RBI	SB
Hargrove, Mike, Clev.*	.317	94	322	43	102	2	49	5
Harlow, Larry, Cal.*	.207	43	82	13	17	0	4	1
Harrah, Toby, Clev.	.291	103	361	64	105	5	44	12
Harris, John, Cal.*	.247	36	77	5	19	3	9	0
Hassey, Ron, Clev.*	.232	61	190	8	44	1	25	0
Hatcher, Mickey, Minn.	.255	99	377	36	96	3	37	3
Hayes, Von, Clev.*	.257	43	109	21	28	1	17	8
Heath, Mike, Oak.	.236	84	301	26	71	8	30	3
Hebner, Richie, Det.*	.226	78	226	19	51	5	28	1
Henderson, Dave, Sea.	.167	59	126	17	21	6	13	2
Henderson, Rickey, Oak.	.319	108	423	89	135	6	35	56
Hisle, Larry, Milw.	.230	27	87	11	20	4	11	0
Hobson, Butch, Cal.	.235	85	268	27	63	4	36	1
Hoffman, Glenn, Bos.	.231	78	242	28	56	1	20	0
Howell, Roy, Milw.*	.238	76	244	37	58	6	33	0
Hrbek, Kent, Minn.*	.239	24	67	5	16	1	7	0
Hurdle, Clint, K.C.*	.329	28	76	12	25	4	15	0
Iorg, Garth, Tor.	.242	70	215	17	52	0	10	2
Jackson, Reggie, N.Y.*	.237	94	334	33	79	15	54	0
Jackson, Ron, Minn.-Det.	.270	85	270	29	73	5	40	6
Johnson, Cliff, Oak.	.260	84	273	40	71	17	59	5
Johnson, Lamar, Chi.	.276	41	134	10	37	1	15	0
Jones, Lynn, Det.	.259	71	174	19	45	2	19	1
Kelleher, Mick, Det.	.221	61	77	10	17	0	6	0
Kelly, Pat, Clev.*	.213	48	75	8	16	1	16	2
Kemp, Steve, Det.*	.277	105	372	52	103	9	49	9
Kuiper, Duane, Clev.*	.257	72	206	15	53	0	14	1
Lansford, Carney, Bos.	.336	102	399	61	134	4	52	15
LeFlore, Ron, Chi.	.246	82	337	46	83	0	24	36
Leach, Rick, Det.*	.193	54	83	9	16	1	11	0
Lemon, Chet, Chi.	.302	94	328	50	99	9	50	5
Lowenstein, John, Balt.*	.249	83	189	19	47	6	20	7
Luzinski, Greg, Chi.	.265	104	378	55	100	21	62	0
Lynn, Fred, Cal.*	.219	76	256	28	56	5	31	1
Macha, Ken, Tor.	.200	37	85	4	17	0	6	1
Mackanin, Pete, Minn.	.231	77	225	21	52	4	18	1
Manning, Rick, Clev.*	.244	103	360	47	88	4	33	25
Martinez, Buck, Tor.	.227	45	128	13	29	4	21	1
Mayberry, John, Tor.*	.248	94	290	34	72	17	43	1

Batter and Club	AVG	G	AB	R	H	HR	RBI	SB
McKay, Dave, Oak.†	.263	79	224	25	59	4	21	4
McRae, Hal, K.C.	.272	101	389	38	106	7	36	3
Mendoza, Mario, Tex.	.231	88	229	18	53	0	22	2
Meyer, Dan, Sea.*	.262	83	252	26	66	3	22	4
Milbourne, Larry, N.Y.†	.313	61	163	24	51	1	12	2
Miller, Rick, Bos.*	.291	97	316	38	92	2	33	3
Molitor, Paul, Milw.	.267	64	251	45	67	2	19	10
Money, Don, Milw.	.216	60	185	17	40	2	14	0
Moore, Charlie, Milw.	.301	48	156	16	47	1	9	1
Morales, Jose, Balt.	.244	38	86	6	21	2	14	0
Morrison, Jim, Chi.	.234	90	290	27	68	10	34	3
Moseby, Lloyd, Tor.*	.233	100	378	36	88	9	43	11
Motley, Darryl, K.C.	.232	42	125	15	29	2	8	1
Mumphrey, Jerry, N.Y.†	.307	80	319	44	98	6	32	13
Murcer, Bobby, N.Y.*	.265	50	117	14	31	6	24	0
Murphy, Dwayne, Oak.*	.251	107	390	58	98	15	60	10
Murray, Eddie, Balt.†	.294	99	378	57	111	22	78	2
Narron, Jerry, Sea.*	.222	76	203	13	45	3	17	0
Nettles, Graig, N.Y.*	.244	103	349	46	85	15	46	0
Newman, Jeff, Oak.	.231	68	216	17	50	3	15	0
Nordhagen, Wayne, Chi.	.308	65	208	19	64	6	33	0
Oglivie, Ben, Milw.*	.243	107	400	53	97	14	72	2
Oliver, Al, Tex.*	.309	102	421	53	130	4	55	3
Orta, Jorge, Clev.*	.272	88	338	50	92	5	34	4
Otis, Amos, K.C.	.269	99	372	49	100	9	57	16
Ott, Ed, Cal.*	.217	75	258	20	56	2	22	2
Paciorek, Tom, Sea.	.326	104	405	50	132	14	66	13
Page, Mitchell, Oak.*	.141	34	92	9	13	4	13	2
Papi, Stan, Det.	.204	40	93	8	19	3	12	1
Parrish, Lance, Det.	.244	96	348	39	85	10	46	2
Perez, Tony, Bos.	.252	84	306	35	77	9	39	0
Peters, Rick, Det.†	.256	63	207	26	53	0	15	1
Picciolo, Rob, Oak.	.268	82	179	23	48	4	13	0
Piniella, Lou, N.Y.	.277	60	159	16	44	5	18	0
Poquette,Tom,Bos.-Tex.*	.152	33	66	2	10	0	7	0
Powell, Hosken, Minn.*	.239	80	264	30	63	2	25	7
Pryor, Greg, Chi.	.224	47	76	4	17	0	6	0
Putnam, Pat, Tex.*	.266	95	297	33	79	8	35	4
Quirk, Jamie, K.C.*	.250	46	100	8	25	0	10	0

Batter and Club	AVG	G	AB	R	H	HR	RBI	SB
Randle, Len, Sea.†	.231	82	273	22	63	4	25	11
Randolph, Willie, N.Y.	.232	93	357	59	83	2	24	14
Remy, Jerry, Bos.*	.307	88	358	55	110	0	31	9
Revering, D., Oak.-N.Y.*	.233	76	206	20	48	4	17	0
Rice, Jim, Bos	.284	108	451	51	128	17	62	2
Rivers, Mickey, Tex.*	.286	99	399	62	114	3	26	9
Roberts, Leon, Tex.	.279	72	233	26	65	4	31	3
Roenicke, Gary, Balt.	.269	85	219	31	59	3	20	1
Romero, Ed, Milw	.198	44	91	6	18	1	10	0
Rosello, Dave, Clev.	.238	43	84	11	20	1	7	0
Rudi, Joe, Bos	.180	49	122	14	22	6	24	0
Sakata, Lenn, Balt	.227	61	150	19	34	5	15	4
Sample, Billy, Tex	.283	66	230	36	65	3	25	4
Serna, Paul, Sea.	.255	30	94	11	24	4	9	2
Simmons, Ted, Milw.†	.216	100	380	45	82	14	61	0
Simpson, Joe, Sea.*	.222	91	288	32	64	2	30	12
Singleton, Ken, Balt.†	.278	103	363	48	101	13	49	0
Smalley, Roy, Minn.†	.263	56	167	24	44	7	22	0
Sofield, Rick, Minn.*	.176	41	102	9	18	0	5	3
Spencer, Jim, N.Y.-Oak.*	.188	79	234	20	44	4	13	1
Squires, Mike, Chi.*	.265	92	294	35	78	0	25	7
Stanley, Fred, Oak.	.193	66	145	15	28	0	7	2
Stapleton, Dave, Bos.	.285	93	355	45	101	10	42	0
Stein, Bill, Tex.	.330	53	115	21	38	2	22	1
Summers, Champ, Det.*	.255	64	165	16	42	3	21	1
Sundberg, Jim, Tex	.277	102	339	42	94	3	28	2
Thomas, Gorman, Milw.	.259	103	363	54	94	21	65	4
Thornton, Andre, Clev.	.239	69	226	22	54	6	30	3
Trammell, Alan, Det.	.258	105	392	52	101	2	31	10
Upshaw, Willie, Tor.*	.171	61	111	15	19	4	10	2
Velez, Otto, Tor	.213	80	240	32	51	11	28	0
Veryzer, Tom, Clev	.244	75	221	13	54	0	14	1
Wagner, Mark, Tex.	.259	50	85	15	22	1	14	1
Ward, Gary, Minn.	.264	85	295	42	78	3	29	5
Washington, Ron, Minn.	.226	28	84	8	19	0	5	4
Washington, U.L., K.C.†	.227	98	339	40	77	2	29	10
Wathan, John, K.C	.252	89	301	24	76	1	19	11
Watson, Bob, N.Y	.212	59	156	15	33	6	12	0
Wells, Greg, Tor	.247	32	73	7	18	0	5	0

Batter and Club	AVG	G	AB	R	H	HR	RBI	SB
Whitaker, Lou, Det.*	.263	109	335	48	88	5	36	5
White, Frank, K.C.	.250	94	364	35	91	9	38	4
Whitt, Ernie, Tor.*	.236	74	195	16	46	1	16	5
Wilfong, Rob, Minn.*	.246	93	305	32	75	3	19	2
Wills, Bump, Tex.†	.251	102	410	51	103	2	41	12
Wilson, Willie, K.C.†	.303	102	439	54	133	1	32	34
Winfield, Dave, N.Y.	.294	105	388	52	114	13	68	11
Wockenfuss, John, Det.	.215	70	172	20	37	9	25	0
Woods, Al, Tor.*	.247	85	288	20	71	1	21	3
Wynegar, Butch, Minn.†	.247	47	150	11	37	0	10	0
Yastrzemski, Carl, Bos.*	.246	91	338	36	83	7	53	0
Yount, Robin, Milw.	.273	96	377	50	103	10	49	4
Zisk, Richie, Sea.	.311	94	357	42	111	16	43	0

AMERICAN LEAGUE

Pitching

(40 or more innings)

***Pitches Left-handed**

*Throws Lefthanded

Pitchers and Club	W	L	ERA	G	IP	H	BB	SO
Aase, Don, Cal	4	4	2.35	39	65	56	24	38
Abbott, Glenn, Sea	4	9	3.95	22	130	127	28	35
Allard, Brian, Sea	3	2	3.75	7	48	48	8	20
Anderson, Larry, Sea	3	3	2.65	41	68	57	18	40
Arroyo, Fernando, Minn	7	10	3.94	23	128	144	34	39
Augustine, Jerry, Milw.*	2	2	4.28	27	61	75	18	26
Bannister, Floyd, Sea*	9	9	4.46	21	121	128	39	85
Barker, Len, Clev	8	7	3.92	22	154	150	46	127
Baumgarten, Ross, Chi*	5	9	4.06	19	102	101	40	52
Beattie, Jim, Sea	3	2	2.96	13	67	59	18	36
Berenguer, Juan, K.C.-Tor	2	13	5.24	20	91	84	51	49
Bird, Doug, N.Y.	5	1	2.72	17	53	58	16	28
Blyeven, Bert, Clev	11	7	2.89	20	159	145	40	107
Bomback, Mark, Tor	5	5	3.90	20	90	84	35	33
Brennan, Tom, Clev	2	2	3.19	7	48	49	14	15
Burgmeier, Tom, Bos*	4	5	2.85	32	60	61	17	35
Burns, Britt, Chi*	10	6	2.64	24	157	139	49	108

*Throws Lefthanded

Pitchers and Club	W	L	ERA	G	IP	H	BB	SO
Caldwell, Mike, Milw*	11	9	3.94	24	144	151	38	41
Campbell, Bill, Bos	1	1	3.19	30	48	45	20	37
Clancy, Jim, Tor	6	12	4.90	22	125	126	64	56
Clark, Bryan, Sea*	2	5	4.35	29	93	92	55	52
Clay, Kenny, Sea	2	7	4.63	22	101	116	42	32
Clear, Mark, Bos	8	3	4.09	34	77	69	51	82
Cleveland, Reggie, Milw	2	3	5.12	35	65	57	30	18
Comer, Steve, Tex	8	2	2.57	36	77	70	31	22
Cooper, Don, Minn	1	5	4.27	27	59	61	32	33
Corbett, Doug, Minn	2	6	2.56	54	88	80	34	60
Crawford, Steve, Bos	0	5	4.97	14	58	69	18	29
Darwin, Danny, Tex	9	9	3.64	22	146	115	57	98
Davis, Ron, N.Y.	4	5	2.71	43	73	47	25	83
Denny, John, Clev	10	6	3.14	19	146	139	66	94
Dotson, Richard, Chi	9	8	3.77	24	141	145	49	73
Drago, Dick, Sea	4	6	5.50	39	54	71	15	27
Easterly, Jamie, Milw*	3	3	3.19	44	62	46	34	31
Eckersley, Dennis, Bos	9	8	4.27	23	154	160	35	79
Erickson, Roger, Minn	3	8	3.86	14	91	93	31	44
Farmer, Ed, Chi	3	3	4.58	42	53	53	34	42
Fingers, Rollie, Milw	6	3	1.04	47	78	55	13	61
Flanagan, Mike, Balt*	9	6	4.19	20	116	108	37	72
Ford, Dave, Balt	1	2	6.53	15	40	61	10	12
Forsch, Ken, Cal	11	7	2.88	20	153	143	27	55
Frost, Dave, Cal	1	8	5.55	12	47	44	19	16
Gale, Rich, K.C.	6	6	5.38	19	102	107	38	47
Garland, Wayne, Clev	3	7	5.79	12	56	89	14	15
Garvin, Jerry, Tor*	1	2	3.40	35	53	46	23	25
Gleaton, Jerry Don, Sea*	4	7	4.76	20	85	88	38	31
Gossage, Rich, N.Y.	3	2	.77	32	47	22	14	18
Guidry, Ron, N.Y.*	11	5	2.76	23	27	100	26	104
Gura, Larry, K.C.*	11	8	2.72	23	72	139	35	61
Haas, Moose, Milw	11	7	4.47	24	37	146	40	64
Hassler, Andy, Cal*	4	3	3.20	42	76	72	33	44
Havens, Brad, Minn*	3	6	3.58	14	78	76	24	43
Hickey, Kevin, Chi*	0	2	3.68	41	44	38	18	17
Honeycutt, Rick, Tex*	11	6	3.30	20	128	120	17	40
Hough, Charlie, Tex	4	1	2.96	21	82	61	31	69

*Throws Lefthanded

Pitcher and Club	W	L	ERA	G	IP	H	BB	SO
Hoyt, Lamarr, Chi	9	3	3.56	43	91	80	28	60
Jackson, Roy, Tor	1	2	2.61	39	62	65	25	27
Jefferson, Jesse, Cal	2	4	3.62	26	77	80	24	27
Jenkins, Fergie, Tex	5	8	4.50	19	106	122	40	63
John, Tommy, N.Y.*	9	8	2.64	20	140	135	39	50
Jones, Jeff, Oak	4	1	3.39	33	61	51	40	43
Jones, Mike, K.C.*	6	3	3.20	12	76	74	28	29
Keough, Matt, Oak	10	6	3.41	19	140	125	45	60
Kingman, Brian, Oak	3	6	3.96	18	100	112	32	52
Kison, Bruce, Cal	1	1	3.48	11	44	40	14	19
Koosman, Jerry, Minn-Chi*	4	13	4.02	27	121	125	41	76
LaRoche, Dave, N.Y.*	4	1	2.49	26	47	38	16	24
Lamp, Dennis, Chi	7	6	2.41	27	127	103	43	71
Langford, Rick, Oak	12	10	3.00	24	195	190	58	84
Leal, Luis, Tor	7	13	3.67	29	130	127	44	71
Leonard, Dennis, K.C.	13	11	2.99	26	202	202	41	107
Lerch, Randy, Milw*	7	9	4.30	23	111	134	43	53
Lopez, Aurelio, Det	5	2	3.62	29	82	70	31	53
Martin, Renie, K.C.	4	5	2.76	29	62	55	29	25
Martinez, Dennis, Balt	14	5	3.32	25	179	173	62	88
Martinez, Tippy, Balt*	3	3	2.90	37	59	48	32	50
Matlack, Jon, Tex*	4	7	4.15	17	104	101	41	43
May, Rudy, N.Y.*	6	11	4.14	27	148	137	41	79
McCatty, Steve, Oak	14	7	2.32	22	186	140	61	91
McGregor, Scott, Balt.*	13	5	3.26	24	160	167	40	82
McLaughlin, Joey, Tor	1	5	2.85	40	60	55	21	38
Medich, Doc, Tex	10	6	3.08	20	143	136	33	65
Monge, Sid, Clev.*	3	5	4.34	31	58	58	21	41
Morris, Jack, Det	14	7	3.05	25	198	153	78	97
Norris, Mike, Oak	12	9	3.75	23	73	145	63	78
Ojeda, Bob, Bos.*	6	2	3.14	10	66	50	25	28
Palmer, Jim, Balt	7	8	3.76	22	27	117	46	35
Parrott, Mike, Sea	3	6	5.08	24	85	102	28	43
Petry, Dan, Det	10	9	3.00	23	141	115	57	79
Quisenberry, Dan, K.C.	1	4	1.74	40	62	59	15	20
Rainey, Chuck, Bos	0	1	2.70	11	40	39	13	20
Rawley, Shane, Sea.*	4	6	3.97	46	68	64	38	35
Redfern, Pete, Minn	9	8	4.06	24	142	140	52	77

*Throws Lefthanded

Pitchers and Club	W	L	ERA	G	IP	H	BB	SO
Renko, Steve, Cal	8	4	3.44	22	102	93	42	50
Reuschel, Rick, N.Y.	4	4	2.66	12	71	75	10	22
Righetti, Dave, N.Y.*	8	4	2.06	15	105	75	38	89
Rozema, Dave, Det	5	5	3.63	28	104	99	25	46
Schatzeder, Dan, Det.*	6	8	6.08	17	71	74	29	20
Slaton, Jim, Milw	5	7	4.38	24	117	120	50	47
Spillner, Dan, Clev	4	4	3.15	32	97	86	39	59
Splittorff, Paul, K.C.*	5	5	4.36	21	99	111	23	48
Stanley, Bob, Bos	10	8	3.82	35	99	110	38	28
Standon, Mike, Clev	3	3	4.40	24	43	43	18	34
Stewart, Sammy, Balt	4	8	2.33	29	112	89	57	57
Stieb, Dave, Tor	11	10	3.18	25	184	148	61	89
Stone, Steve, Balt	4	7	4.57	15	63	63	27	30
Tanana, Frank, Bos.*	4	10	4.02	24	141	142	43	78
Tobik, Dave, Det	2	2	2.70	27	141	142	43	78
Todd, Jackson, Tor	2	7	3.95	21	98	94	31	41
Torrez, Mike, Bos	10	3	3.69	22	127	130	51	54
Trout, Steve, Chi.*	8	7	3.46	20	125	122	38	54
Tudor, John, Bos.*	4	3	4.56	18	79	74	28	44
Underwood, T., N.Y. Oak.*	4	6	3.64	25	84	69	38	75
Verhoeven, John, Minn.	0	0	3.98	25	52	57	14	16
Vuckovich, Pete, Milw	14	4	3.54	24	150	137	57	84
Waits, Rick, Clev.*	8	10	4.93	22	126	173	44	51
Wilcox, Milt, Det	12	9	3.04	24	166	152	52	79
Williams, Al, Minn	6	10	4.08	23	150	160	52	76
Witt, Mike, Cal	8	9	3.28	22	129	123	47	75
Wright, Jim, K.C.	2	3	3.46	17	52	57	21	27
Zahn, Geoff, Cal.*	10	11	4.42	25	161	181	43	52

NATIONAL LEAGUE

Batting

(60 or more at-bats)

***Bats Left-handed** **†Switch-hitter**

Player & Club	AVG	G	AB	R	HR	RBI	SB
Aguayo, Luis, Phil.	.214	45	84	11	1	7	1
Alexander, Doyle, S.F.	.176	24	51	5	0	6	0
Alexander, Gary, Pitt.	.213	21	47	6	1	6	0
Ashby, Alan, Hou.#	.271	83	255	20	4	33	0

Player & Club	AVG	G	AB	R	HR	RBI	SB
Asselstine, Brian, Atl.*	.256	56	86	8	2	10	1
Bailor, Robert, N.Y.	.284	51	81	11	0	8	2
Baker, Johnnie, L.A.	.320	103	400	48	9	49	10
Bass, Randy, S.D.*	.210	69	176	13	4	20	0
Bench, Johnny, Cin.	.309	52	178	14	8	25	0
Benedict, Bruce, Atl.	.264	90	295	26	5	35	1
Berenyi, Bruce, Cin.	.190	21	42	4	0	1	0
Bergman, David, Hou.-S.F.*	.252	69	151	17	4	14	2
Berra, Dale, Pitt.	.241	81	232	21	2	27	11
Biittner, Larry, Cin.*	.213	42	61	1	0	8	0
Blackwell, Timothy, Chi.#	.234	58	158	21	1	11	2
Boggs, Thomas, Atl.	.152	25	46	2	0	3	0
Bonds, Bobby, Chi.	.215	45	163	26	6	19	5
Bonilla, Juan, S.D.	.290	99	369	30	1	25	4
Boone, Robert, Phil.	.211	76	227	19	4	24	2
Bowa, Lawrence, Phil.#	.283	103	360	34	0	31	16
Braun, Stephen, St.L.*	.196	44	46	9	0	2	1
Brenley, Robert, S.F.	.333	19	45	5	1	4	0
Brooks, Hunter, N.Y.	.307	98	358	34	4	38	9
Buckner, William, Chi.*	.311	106	421	45	10	75	5
Butler, Brett, Atl.*	.254	40	126	17	0	4	9
Cabell, Enos, S.F.	.255	96	396	41	2	36	6
Carlton, Steve, Phil.*	.134	24	67	5	0	4	0
Carter, Gary, Mtl.	.251	100	374	48	16	68	1
Cedeno, Cesar, Hou.	.271	82	306	42	5	34	12
Cey, Ronald, L.A.	.288	85	312	42	13	50	0
Chambliss, C. Chris., Atl.*	.272	107	404	44	8	51	4
Clark, Jack, S.F.	.268	99	385	60	17	53	1
Collins, David, Cin.#	.272	95	360	63	3	23	26
Concepcion, David, Cin.	.306	106	421	57	5	67	4
Cromartie, Warren, Mtl.*	.304	99	358	41	6	42	2
Cruz, Hector, Chi.	.229	53	109	15	7	15	2
Cruz, Jose, Hou.*	.267	107	409	53	13	55	5
Cubbage, Michael, N.Y.*	.213	67	80	9	1	4	0
Davis, Jody, Chi.	.256	56	180	14	4	21	0
Davis, Richard, Phil.	.333	45	96	12	2	19	1
Dawson, Andre, Mtl.	.302	103	394	71	24	64	26
DeJesus, Ivan, Chi.	.194	106	403	49	0	13	21
Dillard, Stephen, Chi.	.218	53	119	18	2	11	0

Player & Club	AVG	G	AB	R	HR	RBI	SB
Driessen, Daniel, Cin.*	.236	82	233	35	7	33	2
Durham, Leon, Chi.*	.290	87	328	42	10	35	25
Easler, Michael, Pitt.*	.286	95	339	43	7	42	4
Edwards, David, S.D.	.214	58	112	13	2	13	3
Eichelberger, Juan, S.D.	.087	25	46	1	0	0	0
Evans, Barry, S.D.	.323	54	93	11	0	7	2
Evans, Darrell, S.F.*	.258	102	357	51	12	48	2
Flannery, Timothy, S.D.*	.254	37	67	4	0	6	1
Fletcher, Scott, Chi.	217	19	46	6	0	1	0
Flynn, R. Douglas, N.Y.	.222	105	325	24	1	20	1
Foli, Timothy, Pitt.	.247	86	316	32	0	20	7
Forsch, Robert, ST.L.	.122	20	41	0	0	3	0
Foster, George, Cin.	.295	108	414	64	22	90	4
Francona, Terry, Mtl.*	.274	34	95	11	1	8	1
Garcia, Alfonso, Hou.	.272	48	136	9	0	15	2
Gardenhire, Ronald, N.Y.	.271	27	48	2	0	3	2
Garner, Philip, Pitt.-Hou.	.248	87	294	35	1	26	10
Garvey, Steven, L.A.	.283	110	431	63	10	64	3
Griffey, G. Kenneth, Cin.*	.311	101	396	65	2	34	12
Griffin, Thomas, S.F.	.195	22	41	1	1	5	0
Gross, Gregory, Phil.*	.225	83	102	14	0	7	2
Guerrero, Pedro, L.A.	.300	98	347	46	12	48	5
Gullickson, William, Mtl.	.152	22	46	1	0	1	0
Harper, Terry, Atl.	.260	40	73	9	2	8	5
Heep, Daniel, Hou.*	.250	33	96	6	0	11	0
Henderson, Stephen, Chi.	.293	82	287	32	5	35	5
Hendrick, George, St.L.	.284	101	394	67	18	61	4
Hernandez, Keith, St.L.*	.306	103	376	65	8	48	12
Herndon, Larry, S.F.	.288	96	364	48	5	41	15
Herr, Thomas, St.L.#	.268	103	411	50	0	46	23
Hodges, Ronald, N.Y.*	.302	35	43	5	1	6	1
Hooton, Burt, L.A.	.190	23	42	3	0	3	0
Horner, J. Robert, Atl.	.277	79	300	42	15	42	2
Householder, Paul, Cin.#	.275	23	69	12	2	9	3
Howe, Arthur, Hou.	.296	103	361	43	3	36	1
Hubbard, Glenn, Atl.	.235	99	361	39	6	33	4
Iorg, Dane, St.L.*	.327	75	217	23	2	39	2
Ivie, Michael, S.F.-Hou.	.254	26	59	3	0	9	0
Johnstone, John, L.A.*	.205	61	83	8	3	6	0

Player & Club	AVG.	G	AB	R	HR	RBI	SB
Jones, Ruppert, S.D.*	.249	105	397	53	4	39	7
Jorgensen, Michael, N.Y.*	.205	86	122	8	3	15	4
Kennedy, Junior, Cin.	.250	27	44	5	0	5	0
Kennedy, Terrence, S.D.*	.301	101	382	32	2	41	0
Kingman, David, N.Y.	.221	100	353	40	2	59	6
Knepper, Robert, Hou.*	.149	22	47	3	1	3	0
Knight, C. Ray, Cin.	.259	106	386	43	6	34	2
Krukow, Michael, Chi.	.180	25	50	5	0	3	0
Lacy, Leondaus, Pitt.	.268	78	213	31	2	10	24
Landestoy, R., Hou.-Cin.#	.153	47	85	8	0	5	5
Landreaux, Kenneth, L.A.*	.251	99	390	48	7	41	18
Landrum, Terry, St.L.	.261	81	119	13	0	10	4
Law, Vance, Pitt.	.134	30	67	1	0	3	1
Lefebvre, Joseph, S.D.*	.256	86	246	31	8	31	6
Lemaster, Johnnie, S.F.	.253	104	324	27	0	28	3
Leonard, Jeffrey, Hou.-S.F.	.290	44	145	21	4	29	5
Lezcano, Sixto, St.L.	.266	72	214	26	5	28	0
Linares, Ruffino, Atl.	.265	78	253	27	5	25	8
Lopes, David, L.A.	.206	58	214	35	5	17	20
Lum, Michael, Atl.-Chi.*	.217	51	69	6	2	7	0
Maddox, Garry, Phil.	.263	94	323	37	5	40	0
Madlock, Bill, Pitt.	.341	82	279	35	6	45	18
Martin, Jerry, S.F.	.241	72	241	23	4	25	6
Matthews, Gary, Phil.	.301	101	359	62	9	67	15
May, Milton, S.F.*	.310	97	316	20	2	33	1
Mazzilli, Lee, N.Y.#	.228	95	324	36	6	34	17
McBride, Arnold, Phil.*	.271	58	221	26	2	21	5
Mejias, Samuel, Cin.	.286	66	49	6	0	7	1
Miller, Edward, Atl.#	.231	50	134	29	0	7	23
Milner, John, Pitt.-Mtl.*	.237	65	135	12	5	18	0
Monday, Robert, L.A.*	.315	66	130	24	11	25	1
Montanez, G., Mtl.-Pitt.*	.210	55	100	8	1	6	0
Morales, Julio, Chi.	.286	84	245	27	1	25	1
Moreland, B. Keith, Phil.	.255	61	196	16	6	37	1
Moreno, Jose, S.D.#	.229	34	48	5	0	6	4
Moreno, Omar, Pitt.*	.276	103	434	62	1	35	39
Morgan, Joe, S.F.*	.240	90	308	47	8	31	14
Mura, Stephen, S.D.	.136	24	44	2	0	4	0
Murphy, Dale, Atl.	.247	104	369	43	13	50	14

Player & Club	AVG.	G	AB	R	HR	RBI	SB
Nicosia, Steven, Pitt.	.231	54	169	21	2	18	3
Niekro, Joseph, Hou.	.176	24	51	1	0	6	0
Niekro, Philip, Atl.	.077	22	52	1	0	1	0
Nolan, Joseph, Cin.*	.309	81	236	25	1	26	1
North, William, S.F.#	.221	46	131	22	1	12	26
O'Berry, P. Michael, Cin.	.180	55	111	6	1	5	0
Oberkfell, Kenneth, St.L.*	.293	102	376	43	2	45	13
Oester, Ronald, Cin.#	.271	105	354	45	5	42	2
Office, Rowland, Mtl.*	.175	26	40	4	0	0	0
Parker, David, Pitt.*	.258	67	240	29	9	48	6
Parrish, Larry, Mtl.	.244	97	349	41	8	44	0
Pastore, Frank, Cin.	.114	22	44	1	0	1	0
Pena, Antonio, Pitt.	.300	66	210	16	2	17	1
Perkins, Broderick, S.D.*	.280	92	254	27	2	40	0
Perry, Gaylord, Atl.	.250	24	48	5	1	7	0
Phillips, Michael, S.D.-Mtl.*	.214	48	84	6	0	4	1
Pittman, Joseph, Hou.	.281	52	135	11	0	7	4
Pocoroba, Biff, Atl.*	.180	57	122	4	0	8	0
Porter, Darrell, St.L.*	.224	61	174	22	6	31	1
Puhl, Terry, Hou.*	.251	96	350	43	3	28	22
Pujols, Luis, Hou.	.239	40	117	5	1	14	1
Raines, Timothy, Mtl.#	.304	88	313	61	5	37	71
Ramirez, Rafael, Atl.	.218	95	307	30	2	20	7
Ramos, Roberto, Mtl.	.195	26	41	4	1	3	0
Ramsey, Michael, St.L.#	.258	47	124	19	0	9	4
Ray, John, Pitt.#	.245	31	102	10	0	6	0
Reitz, Kenneth, Chi.	.215	82	260	10	2	28	0
Reuss, Jerry, L.A.*	.196	22	51	3	0	3	0
Reynolds, G. Craig, Hou.*	.260	87	323	43	4	31	3
Rhoden, Richard, Pitt.	.188	21	48	4	0	0	0
Richards, Eugene, S.D.*	.288	104	393	47	3	42	20
Roberts, David, Hou.	.241	27	54	4	1	5	1
Robinson, William, Pitt.	.216	39	88	8	2	8	1
Roenicke, Ronald, L.A.#	.234	22	47	6	0	0	1
Rogers, Stephen, Mtl.	.145	23	55	5	0	3	0
Roof, Eugene, St.L.#	.300	23	60	11	0	3	5
Rose, Peter, Phil.#	.325	107	431	73	0	33	4
Royster, Jeron, Atl.	.204	64	93	13	0	9	7
Russell, William, L.A.	.233	82	262	20	0	22	2

Player & Club	AVG.	G	AB	R	HR	RBI	SB
Ruthven, Richard, Phil.	.140	23	50	2	0	5	0
Ryan, L. Nolan, Hou.	.216	21	51	3	0	1	0
Salazar, Luis, S.D.	.303	109	400	37	3	38	11
Sanchez, Orlando, St.L.*	.286	27	49	5	0	6	1
Sax, Stephen, L.A.	.277	31	119	15	2	9	5
Schmidt, Michael, Phil.	.316	102	354	78	31	91	12
Scioscia, Michael, L.A.*	.276	93	290	27	2	29	0
Scott, Michael, N.Y.	.073	23	41	4	0	1	0
Scott, Rodney, Mtl.#	.205	95	336	43	0	26	30
Scott, Tony, St.L.-Hou.#	.264	100	401	49	4	39	18
Seaver, G. Thomas, Cin.	.200	23	55	3	1	6	0
Smith, Billy, S.F.#	.180	36	61	6	1	5	0
Smith, Lonnie, Phil.	.324	62	176	40	2	11	21
Smith, Osborne, S.D.#	.222	110	450	53	0	21	22
Solomon, Eddie, Pitt.	.163	25	43	3	0	3	0
Sorensen, Lary, St.L.	.065	23	46	1	0	0	0
Soto, Mario, Cin.	.068	25	59	4	0	0	0
Speier, Chris, Mtl.	.225	96	307	33	2	25	1
Spilman, W. H., Cin.-Hou.*	.241	51	58	9	0	4	0
Stargell, Wilver, Pitt.*	.283	38	60	2	0	9	0
Staub, Daniel, N.Y.*	.317	70	161	9	5	21	1
Stearns, John, N.Y.	.271	80	273	25	1	24	12
Stennett, Renaldo, S.F.	.230	38	87	8	1	7	2
Strain, Joseph, Chi.	.189	25	74	7	0	1	0
Sutton, Donald, Hou.	.137	23	51	1	0	3	0
Tabler, Patrick, Chi.	.188	35	101	11	1	5	0
Traveras, Franklin, N.Y.	.230	84	283	30	0	11	16
Templeton, Garry, St.L.#	.288	80	333	47	1	33	8
Tenance, F. Gene, St.L.	.233	58	129	26	5	22	0
Thomas, Derrel, L.A.#	.248	80	218	25	4	24	7
Thompson, Jason, Pitt.*	.242	86	223	36	15	42	0
Thompson, V. Scot, Chi.*	.165	57	115	8	0	8	2
Thon, Richard, Hou.	.274	49	95	13	0	3	6
Tracy, James, Chi.*	.238	45	63	6	0	5	1
Trevino, Alejandro, N.Y.	.262	56	149	17	0	10	3
Trillo, J. Manuel, Phil.	.287	94	349	37	6	36	10
Tyson, Michael, Chi.#	.185	50	92	6	2	8	1
Unser, Delbert, Phil.*	.153	62	59	5	0	6	0
Valentine, Ellis, Mtl.-N.Y.	.208	70	245	23	8	36	0

Player & Club	AVG	G	AB	R	HR	RBI	SB
Valenzuela, Fernando, L.A.*	.250	25	64	3	0	7	0
Wallach, Timothy, Mtl.	.236	71	212	19	4	13	0
Waller, E. Tyrone, Chi.	.268	30	71	10	3	13	2
Walling, Dennis, Hou.*	.234	65	158	23	5	23	2
Washington, Claudell, Atl.*	.291	85	320	37	5	37	12
Welch, Robert, L.A.	.222	23	45	3	0	2	0
Welsh, Christopher, S.D.*	.146	22	41	4	0	1	0
White, Jerome, Mtl.#	.218	59	119	11	3	11	5
Wilson, William, N.Y.#	.271	92	328	49	3	14	24
Wohlford, James, S.F.	.162	50	68	4	1	7	0
Woods, Gary, Hou.	.209	54	110	10	0	12	2
Yeager, Stephen, L.A.	.209	42	86	5	3	7	0
Youngblood, Joel, N.Y.	.350	43	143	16	4	25	2

NATIONAL LEAGUE

Pitching

(40 or more innings)

***Pitchers Left-handed**

Pitcher & Club	ERA	W	L	G	IP	H	BB	SO
Alexander, Doyle, S.F.	2.90	11	7	24	152	156	44	77
Allen, Neil, N.Y.	2.96	7	6	43	67	64	26	50
Andujar, J., Hou.-St.L. ...	4.10	8	4	20	79	85	23	37
Bahnsen, Stanley, Mtl.	4.96	2	1	25	49	45	24	28
Bair, C. D., Cin.-St.L.	5.07	4	2	35	55	55	19	30
Berenyi, Bruce, Cin.	3.50	9	6	21	126	97	77	106
Bibby, James, Pitt.	2.49	6	3	14	94	79	26	48
Bird, J. Douglas, Chi.	3.60	4	5	12	75	72	16	34
Blue, Vida, S.F.*	2.45	8	6	18	125	97	54	63
Boggs, Thomas, Atl.	4.09	3	13	25	143	140	54	81
Boone, Daniel, S.D.*	2.86	1	0	37	63	63	21	43
Breining, Fred, S.F.	2.54	5	2	45	78	66	38	37
Burris, B. Ray, Mtl.	3.04	9	7	22	136	117	41	52
Bystrom, Martin, Phil.	3.33	4	3	9	54	55	16	24
Camp, Rick, Atl.	1.78	9	3	48	76	68	12	47
Candelaria, John, Pitt.* ...	3.51	2	2	6	41	42	11	14
Capilla, Douglas, Chi.*	3.18	1	0	42	51	52	34	28
Carlton, Steven, Phil.*	2.42	13	4	24	190	152	62	179
Castillo, Robert, L.A.	5.29	2	4	34	51	50	24	35

Pitcher & Club	ERA	W	L	G	IP	H	BB	SO
Caudill, William, Chi.	5.83	1	5	30	71	87	31	45
Christenson, Larry, Phil...	3.53	4	7	20	107	108	30	70
Curtis, John, S.D.*	5.10	2	6	28	67	70	30	31
Davis, Mark, Phil.*.........	7.74	1	4	9	43	49	24	29
Eastwick, Rawlins, Chi. ...	2.30	0	1	30	43	43	15	24
Eichelberger, Juan, S.D...	3.51	8	8	25	141	136	74	81
Espinosa, Arnulfo, Phil....	6.08	2	5	14	74	98	24	22
Falcone, Peter, N.Y.*......	2.56	5	3	35	95	84	36	56
Forsch, Robert St.L........	3.19	10	5	20	124	106	29	41
Fryman, Woodrow, Mtl.* .	1.88	5	3	35	43	38	14	25
Garber, H. Eugene, Atl. ...	2.59	4	6	35	59	49	20	34
Goltz, David, L.A...........	4.09	2	7	26	77	83	25	48
Griffin, Michael, Chi.	4.50	2	5	16	52	64	9	20
Griffin, Thomas, S.F.......	3.77	8	8	22	129	121	57	83
Gullickson, William, Mtl...	2.81	7	9	22	157	142	34	115
Harris, Greg, N.Y.	4.43	3	5	16	69	65	28	54
Holland, Alfred, S.F.*......	2.41	7	5	47	101	87	44	78
Hooton, Burt, L.A..........	2.28	11	6	23	142	124	33	74
Howe, Steve, L.A.*	2.50	5	3	41	54	51	18	32
Hume, Thomas, Cin.	3.44	9	4	51	68	63	31	27
Jackson, Grant, Pitt.-Mtl.*	3.77	2	2	45	43	44	19	21
Jones, Odell, Pitt...........	3.33	4	5	13	54	51	23	30
Jones, Randall, N.Y.*	4.88	1	8	13	59	65	38	14
Kaat, James, St.L.*........	3.40	6	6	41	53	60	17	8
Knepper, Robert, Hou.*...	2.18	9	5	22	157	128	38	75
Kravec, Kenneth, Chi.*	5.08	1	6	24	78	80	39	50
Krukow, Michael, Chi......	3.69	9	9	25	144	146	55	101
LaCorte, Frank, Hou.	3.64	4	2	37	42	41	21	40
LaCoss, Michael, Cin.	6.12	4	7	20	78	102	30	22
Lavelle, Gary, S.F.*	3.82	2	6	34	66	58	23	45
Lea, Charles, Mtl...........	4.64	5	4	16	64	63	26	31
Lee, William, Mtl.*.........	2.93	5	6	31	89	90	14	34
Littell, Mark, St.L.	4.39	1	3	28	41	36	31	22
Littlefield, John, S.D.......	3.66	2	3	42	64	53	28	21
Lollar, W. Timothy, S.D.*	6.08	2	8	24	77	87	51	38
Lucas, Gary, S.D.*.........	2.00	7	7	57	90	78	36	53
Lyle, Albert, Phil.*	4.44	9	6	48	75	85	33	29

Pitcher and Club	ERA	W	L	G	IP	H	BB	SO
Lynch, Edward, N.Y.	2.93	4	5	17	80	79	21	27
Mahler, Richard, Atl.	2.81	8	6	34	112	109	43	54
Martin, John. St.L.*	3.41	8	5	17	103	85	26	36
Martinez, Silvio, St.L	3.99	2	5	18	97	95	39	34
Martz, Randy, Chi..........	3.67	5	7	33	108	103	49	32
McGlothen, Lynn, Chi.	4.75	1	4	20	55	71	28	26
McGraw, Frank, Phil.*.....	2.66	2	4	34	44	35	14	26
Minton, Gregory, S.F......	2.89	4	5	55	84	84	36	29
Montefusco, John, Atl.....	3.51	2	3	26	77	75	27	34
Moskau, Paul, Cin.	4.91	2	1	27	55	54	32	32
Mura, Stephen, S.D.	4.27	5	14	23	139	156	50	70
Niekro, Joseph, Hou.......	2.82	9	9	24	166	150	47	77
Niekro, Philip, Atl.	3.11	7	7	22	139	120	56	62
Noles, Dickie, Phil.	4.19	2	2	13	58	57	23	34
Pastore, Frank, Cin.	4.02	4	9	22	132	125	35	81
Perez, Pascual, Pitt.	3.98	2	7	17	86	92	34	46
Perry, Gaylord, Atl.	3.93	8	9	23	151	182	24	60
Price, Joseph, Cin.*	2.50	6	1	41	54	42	18	41
Proly, Michael, Phil........	3.86	2	1	35	63	66	19	19
Reardon, J., N.Y.-Mtl.	2.19	3	0	43	70	48	21	49
Reed, Ronald, Phil.........	3.10	5	3	39	61	54	17	40
Reuschel, Ricky, Chi.......	3.45	4	7	13	86	87	23	53
Reuss, Jerry, L.A.*	2.29	10	4	22	153	138	27	51
Rhoden, Richard, Pitt.	3.90	9	4	21	136	147	53	76
Ripley, Allen, S.F..........	4.05	4	4	19	91	103	27	47
Rogers, Stephen, Mtl......	3.41	12	8	22	161	149	41	87
Romo, Enrique, Pitt........	4.50	1	3	33	42	47	18	23
Ruhle, Vernon, Hou........	2.91	4	6	20	102	97	20	39
Ruthven, Richard, Phil. ...	5.14	12	7	23	147	162	54	80
Ryan, L. Nolan, Hou.......	1.69	11	5	21	149	99	68	140
Sambito, Joseph, Hou.* ..	1.83	5	5	49	64	43	22	41
Sanderson, Scott, Mtl.	2.96	9	7	22	137	122	31	77
Scott, Michael, N.Y........	3.90	5	10	23	136	130	34	54
Scurry, Rodney, Pitt.*.....	3.77	4	5	27	74	74	40	65
Searage, Raymond, N.Y.*	3.65	1	0	26	37	34	17	16
Seaver, G. Thomas, Cin...	2.55	14	2	23	166	120	66	87
Shirley, Robert, St.L.*	4.10	6	4	28	79	78	34	36
Smith, David, Hou.	2.76	5	3	42	75	54	23	52

Pitchers and Club	ERA	W	L	G	IP	H	BB	SO
Smith, Lee, Chi.............	3.49	3	6	40	67	57	31	50
Solomon, Eddie, Pitt.......	3.12	8	6	22	127	133	27	38
Sorensen, Lary, St.L.	3.28	7	7	23	140	149	26	52
Soto, Mario, Cin............	3.29	12	9	25	175	142	61	151
Stewart, David, L.A........	2.51	4	3	32	43	40	14	29
Sutcliffe, Richard, L.A.....	4.02	2	2	14	47	41	20	16
Sutter, H. Bruce, St.L.....	2.63	3	5	48	82	64	24	57
Sutton, Donald, Hou.......	2.60	11	9	23	159	132	29	104
Tekulve, Kenton, Pitt.	2.49	5	5	45	65	61	17	34
Tiant, Luis, Pitt............	3.95	2	5	9	57	54	19	32
Tidrow, Richard, Chi.......	5.04	3	10	51	75	73	30	39
Urrea, John, S.D...........	2.39	2	2	38	49	43	28	19
Valenzuela, F., L.A.*.......	2.48	13	7	25	192	140	61	180
Walk, Robert, Atl...........	4.60	1	4	12	43	41	23	16
Welch, Robert, L.A.	3.45	9	5	23	141	141	41	88
Welsh, Christopher, S.D.*	3.77	6	7	22	124	122	41	51
Whitson, Eddie, S.F.	4.02	6	9	22	123	130	47	65
Wise, Richard, S.D.	3.77	4	8	18	98	116	19	27
Zachry, Patrick, N.Y.	4.14	7	14	24	139	151	56	76

LATE NEWS

The Houston Astros traded 1B-OF Cesar Cedeno to the Cincinnati Reds for 3B Ray Knight.

The New York Yankees signed free-agent 1B-OF Dave Collins, formerly of Cincinnati.

The Minnesota Twins traded OF Hosken Powell to the Toronto Blue Jays for 1B Boomer Wells.

Toronto sent P Paul Mirabella to the Chicago Cubs for a player to be named.

Cleveland traded IF Tom Veryzer to the Mets for P Ray Searage.

Minnesota traded C Scott Madison and P Paul Voigt to the Dodgers for P Bobby Castillo and OF Bobby Mitchell.

Kansas City signed free-agent OF Tom Poquette.

California signed free-agent OF Reggie Jackson.

Montreal traded P Grant Jackson to the Royals for 1B Ken Phelps.

Montreal signed free-agent C Tim Blackwell.

Philadelphia traded SS Larry Bowa and IF Ryne Sandberg to the Chicago Cubs for SS Ivan DeJesus.